The
Shakespeare
Toolkit

A Nuts-and-Bolts Approach to Speaking Shakespeare

Brian A. Rose
Adelphi University

WAVELAND
PRESS, INC.
Long Grove, Illinois

For information about this book, contact:
Waveland Press, Inc.
4180 IL Route 83, Suite 101
Long Grove, IL 60047-9580
(847) 634-0081
info@waveland.com
www.waveland.com

10-digit ISBN 1-4786-4877-5
13-digit ISBN 978-1-4786-4877-2

Printed in the United States of America

7 6 5 4 3 2 1

Contents

A Short Preface

It's fitting that a nuts-and-bolts approach to speaking Shakespeare should have been inspired by a genuine nut-and-bolt.

I was doing some work at Cornell. A PhD student in chemistry lived across the street; our kids were the same age and we'd become friends. I found him on his porch one morning, tossing something casually up and down with an air of satisfaction. He handed it to me; it was a perfectly machined two-inch bolt with a complex carved nut that spun with no sound or resistance. The nut and bolt both had a small hole drilled through them that took a pin, locking the nut into place. It was a delightfully efficient object, wonderfully machined. He told me with some pride that he had made it out of a small block of metal. His assignment was to make this object to these exact specifications, to carve this perfectly working little machine out of a featureless block of aluminum. I was suitably impressed.

"But your field is chemistry," I asked. "Why are you being trained in metalwork?"

"Because if you are going to do original work, be able to think in new ways, solve problems that no one else has solved or even thought of, the *tools* you need to accomplish the work may not exist! So you have to know how to make the tools you need." It was a revelation, put that way. He gave me the thing. I keep it near the computer.

Some years later, I was asked by Adelphi University's Department of Theatre to teach Shakespearean performance to preprofessional students—a new task for me, and a difficult one. I had been an actor for over twenty years and frequently performed Shakespeare; but how does one turn one's own knowledge, a complex collection of sparks in the brain arranged by experiences and study, into something teachable, and teachable in a relatively short period of time? I needed a "toolkit" that I could use in class and that the students could take away as part of their process for working on their future Shakespeare. I found a lot of useful stuff from a wide range of sources, but no straightforward, coordinated set of ideas that could serve as a foundation for work, and certainly none that was easily learned and capable of being used quickly. I needed a set of ideas functioning as tools, the use of which would build up the actor's confidence to make activated choices, strong choices that embodied the actor's personal choices for the way to play a character more truthfully.

I quickly learned that actors put up their own personal obstacles in the way of the delivery of those truthful readings. I worked with students who didn't pause, didn't choose specific words to strongly stress, or simply kept talking until they began to run out of breath. **I came to think that the solution might be as simple as working with the verse-dialogue as sentences; that is, as thoughts that the character needs to use to make a point. This is, obviously, as true of daily speech as of Shakespeare.**

Hence, the Toolkit. The tools, working together, help the actor to study the common ground shared by daily speech and by Shakespeare's carefully crafted language. This doesn't naturalize away the verse, but helps to make the verse sound more real, more like speech inspired by some inner need. By seeing the verse as sentences embodying thoughts, the actor is freer to speak them as if they were their own; they become less alien as verse and less intimidating than when tagged as "Shakespeare." We already have a mastery of the tools of communication needed to organize and express our intentions, and the Toolkit consciously applies those tools to Shakespeare's virtual people. When we use the tools for our everyday speech, the techniques are internalized, their use unnoticed consciously. **When we act, we need to use the tools consciously to turn written words into spoken language,** language that creates the "illusion of the first time." As both Hamlet and Stanislavski[1] point out, acting must always hold a mirror up to nature.

I should note that, unlike my friend, I haven't actually *made* these tools. I found them, guided by hints and insights from many areas and

---

1. Constantin Stanislavski was an important creator of a system of naturalistically rooted acting; he was working as an actor, director, and theorist at the Moscow Art Theatre at the end of the nineteenth and into the twentieth centuries.

sources: from the memoirs and suggestions of great actors, from important directors and theorists, from master-teachers of performing Shakespeare, from Elizabethan poets and critics, from today's experts on
meter's forms and uses, and from intonation theorists, experts in why we
use the tones and stresses that we do to communicate.

The Tools and Some Essentials

THE TOOLKIT AND THE TOOLS

The Toolkit is a catchy name for ten useful tips and bits of knowledge related to speaking sentences. They form a "kit" because, like any toolkit, the tools are used individually or together to accomplish specific goals. Some toolkits are for making chairs, some for cooking food or making paintings, but **this Toolkit helps actors craft energetic and more naturalistic readings of dramatic dialogue.** This dialogue represents the thoughts, intentions, and/or needs of a virtual being, as I think of characters. We're working with Shakespeare, and there are specifics relating to him in the Toolkit, but all worthy dramatic dialogue is carefully designed to express specific thoughts, intentions, or needs arising from the unique circumstances of the play. The secret of the Toolkit (if there is one) is that you also do that; you carefully design your spoken thoughts to express the same kinds of needs and intentions, the majority of which are agenda-driven steps in a strategy.

Because this is the case, and because art mirrors life, the Toolkit works for Molière, Marlowe, Fletcher, whomever: it works for any material in blank verse or iambic pentameter. It has to. It's all in sentences. But for our introduction to the tools, we'll focus on how you have already been using the techniques you need to feel confident in speaking Shakespeare.

Stanislavski teaches that acting is rooted in the study of humanity, and that you are, yourself, the best object of study. You're the closest human at hand, and the only one whose mind you have access to. So study yourself. For the time being, it should be a study of **how you create sentences: how do you use intonations, stresses, varied pauses, and**

1

pace (among other things) when you speak? Sometimes I ask my students to do this: set your phone on record and record yourself for the entire day. For the sake of fairness, tell anyone you're chatting with what you're doing and why. At the end of the day, listen to yourself. How do you phrase things? Vary your pace? Use patterns of stresses and tones to answer other people or to initiate an exchange of thoughts on any subject? Note that you always had enough breath to say what you wanted to, were relaxed as you spoke, paused where you needed to or wanted to, used virtual punctuation, and that your intonations were all over the place, busily working away.

So if the Tools sound familiar or seem obvious in use, keep in mind that we use the same tools to play Hamlet as we would to order a pizza. We and our characters craft speech that is meant to have an effect, to manipulate people effectively and to engineer events, always for the fulfillment of our intentions and needs. If you understand more clearly what you already do, and how you do it, then you can use that knowledge consciously on your text.

The Toolkit concept assumes, then, that we can learn to energize our spoken Shakespeare as much by understanding how a character's sentences are put together, as by studying the specifics of language and situation. In an age of psychological realism, this can sound radical or ever reactionary; but great teachers before me encountered this phenomenon, and came to the same "radical" realization. Patsy Rodenburg, one of the greatest performance teachers of voice and Shakespeare in the later twentieth century, tells this tale:

> When I first started teaching in the 1970s, I often came across great actors who admitted that they didn't really understand the content of Shakespeare's speeches, but found a way through by accurately following the form of the verse. At the time, I worked as an apprentice to a brilliant—and slightly terrifying—classical voice coach. Her teaching was based on the same principle. . . . She believed that if you followed form, the emotional and intellectual life written into the text would automatically be released. At first I was skeptical. My own training had been based more in the new way—giving priority to thought and emotion—but I had to acknowledge, while working with that coach and those actors, that a strict observance of form did engage them fully and release the text. . . .
>
> So a full respect for form is nothing new; rather, in our current theatre, it's more like an ancient knowledge in danger of extinction. But

the most important thing to stress about it is this: the knowledge of form is not just an intellectual awareness but one that must be fully incorporated in the voice and body of the actor. Only then will it serve its purpose.[1]

THE TOOLS

Although we must deal with ideas in a linear way, it's important to note that **the tools are all working together, all of the time,** operating for you each day as you speak your own purposeful thoughts. You're not thinking about pausing or stressing or intoning consciously; it happens as it's needed. **And that's the secret of acting: the same things, all of them, happen to the characters, but through you.**

1: THE SENTENCE TOOL

Every sentence spoken or written is the expression of a thought: there are no generic sentences. Make the point of the sentence as strongly and clearly as you can. At the start, don't worry about meter, lines, or verse: read the lines together as parts of sentences.

2: THE PUNCTUATION TOOL

Use punctuation consciously and actively for phrasing, breathing, stressing, pausing, and, very importantly, intonation. Let the punctuation help you string together the pieces of the thought. Remember that intonation is the clearest and most effective way into an audience member's mind.

3: THE STRESS TOOL

Shakespeare's work was meant to be spoken using at least three distinct levels of stress: a light one, a widely ranging middle stress, and the strongest stress. These are flexible and under the actor's control. Remember that there can only be one strongest stress in any sentence. Decide on it and hit it hard: that will help organize meaning and context.

---

1. Patsy Rodenburg, *Speaking Shakespeare* (New York: Palgrave Macmillan, 2004), 70–71.

4: STANISLAVSKI'S STRESS TOOL

Stanislavski says that there are three specific tools in your kit for adding energy and personalized meaning to your work: strong verbal stresses on chosen key words; holding or using vowels to vary duration of words and phrases; and/or the conscious use of persuasive intonation. Ideally, he writes, stress, duration, and intonation should be used in combination.

5: THE SINGLE BEAT WORD TOOL

Pairs or strings of monosyllabic, single-beat words provide opportunities to personalize a line-reading by adding extra strong stresses to lines, and therefore to sentences. The choice by the actor of how to use these extra strong stresses empowers his or her personalization of the energy that has been invested by the writer in meter. Used with the Stress Tool, the actor can control meter with a great deal of command.

6: THE VERB AND PROPER NOUN TOOL

Hit verbs (action words) and capitalized nouns (people, places, or things known to the character) with a strong stress. This creates the illusion of the character's world of action and of personal connections or imagery and adds strong stresses to help energize readings.

7: THE ANTITHESIS TOOL

An antithesis is a juxtaposing of two words, images, phrases, or ideas connected by words like "and," "but," and some others. Shakespeare uses them a great deal; find them and play them strongly and deliberately as an active choice made by the character, usually by adding stronger stress to the second of the pair.

8: THE PAUSE TOOL

There are three lengths of pauses in verse drama that are used for different purposes. As you work, observe consciously how tiny micropauses for phrasing, longer, intoned pauses associated with punctuation, and the filled, transitional pauses between sentences, can be active parts of your toolkit.

9: The Phrasing and Midline Break Tool

English speakers naturally tend to speak in three- to five-word phrases. Micropauses link the phrases into thoughts. Without that phrasing pattern, spoken material sounds memorized. A special phrasing pause that occurs in the middle of a verse line—usually after the fourth, fifth, or sixth beat—is called the midline break. It was put there by Shakespeare to allow a ten-beat line to be handled as two phrases.

10: The End of the Line Tool

Imbue the last beat of the line with energy—don't let the line weaken near its end. The last beat of each line connects to the first beat of the next line; the last word of a line is often a verb, name, key word, or a resolution of meaning, all of which benefit from or require the application of stress; or may be punctuated, each mark of which requires verbal energy of some type.

And those are the Tools. **You probably noticed that you use lots of these in normal speech**: you use multiple levels of stress (about four), you deliberately assign strong stresses to important words, you vary the lengths of pauses and use them to house intonations, etc. **The Tools are meant to draw your attention to your already highly developed ability to deal with Shakespeare.**

Some Essentials

There are some important things to discuss before we plunge into using the Tools. In chapter 2, we first explore how our verbal communication requires the things we call the Tools, and in chapter 3, we'll look at how the Toolkit needs Constantin Stanislavski's ideas. It turns out there are important elements of Stanislavski's System of naturalistic acting that are as important for speaking Shakespeare confidently as knowing how the verse is put together.

Some Basics

When you are ready to use the Toolkit for work on a monologue, role, or scene, in an acting lab or in rehearsal, a few **basics** have to be assumed. **The first** is that you have read the play you are working from, and **the**

second is that you are working from a book with lots of useful notes at the bottom of the page. This is called a **variorum**. A "complete works" is a monstrously sized compendium with few or no notes. Without the notes handy, you have no help in understanding the character's use of vocabulary and imagery, or insight into Elizabethan usages, and much less access to the story details or background information you need to speak your character's words believably. **An important truth about learning to act is that it is more a process of removing obstacles to "doing," than it is a process of "learning to do."** In the case of work on Shakespeare or any of his contemporaries, any ignorance of the information available in the notes is a huge obstacle, but fortunately, an easy one to remove.

The third thing is to always work out loud; read the material silently as many times as you wish, but when working on the material, always do it out loud. You need to do this to explore how breath and body participate in powerful, personalized readings. The **fourth thing is to ban screens from your work** once you have done what research you need to do: do not read/work from phones, tablets, laptops, or any other screen. For serious work, have your text on a piece of paper in your hand, or in a variorum. Always have a pad handy, and pencils—only pencils—for marking text or taking notes. If you are working on a short passage, **memorize it.** Memorize as soon as you can, but **memorize words and intentions, not line-readings.** Students often memorize the line-readings that accompanied their memorization work; to say the least, they are usually underdeveloped.

Memorizing the words is only the first step toward strong acting, not the achievement of it. Now comes the investigation and experimentation, the development of the text/lines/sentences, and using the simple tools to create not-so-simple readings. No one performance of material should be identical to another, nor is that a goal to strive for. A performance is like a train trip taken frequently: the tracks are always the same, but the journeys are always different.

THE MOLIÈRE TRAPS . . .

Poor Jean-Baptiste de Poquelin, better known as **Molière**! He is the second most produced playwright in the world, after you-know-who. The Richard Wilbur translations opened up Molière to Bard-centric English speakers. Wilbur turned Molière's twelve-beat iambic lines into the familiar ten-beat lines of English-language theatre verse. He also preserved Molière's rhyming pattern: AABB, with each pair of lines rhyming.

But in using these texts as ways to teach the playing of iambic and blank verse material, I discovered that **there is a set of traps into which every actor is in danger of falling, and from which there is no escaping back into a naturalistic reading of the verse.** At first, I did not recognize the true and insidious nature of these traps, because they are not **in the text,** but **built into the way English verse-drama is conventionally printed on a page!** But to be forewarned is to be forearmed: by identifying the Molière Traps and how they work, your verse work will be off to a much stronger start.

Here's how the traps work, using a small passage from Wilbur's translation of *Tartuffe*:

> Brother, I don't pretend to be a sage,
> Nor have I all the wisdom of the age.
> There's just one insight I would dare to claim:
> I know that true and false are not the same;
> And just as there is nothing I more revere
> Than a soul whose faith is steadfast and sincere,
> Nothing that I more cherish and admire
> Than honest zeal and true religious fire,
> So there is nothing that I find more base
> Than specious piety's dishonest face . . .

Because the lines are vertically stacked and form a square, and because they are all roughly the same length, three traps emerge: **the meter trap, the pace trap, and the sentence trap.**

An actor falls into the meter trap when they speak the verse with a mechanical use of the meter, **reading it as binary,** with two levels of stress, one lighter than the other. The result is that all of the lines have the same metrical pattern, lack any variety, and sound false. The solutions, we'll discover, lie in widely varying the level of the metrical strikes (the Stress Tool), adding micropauses for phrasing the lines (the Phrasing Tool), and/or exercising your options to hold vowels and fill them with strong intonations (Stanislavski's Stress Tool). The Toolkit's got it covered. It's your personalized mixture of stresses, phrasing, and pacing that enhances the human naturalism underlying the structured verse.

The pace trap is related to the meter trap: because the lines are the same length on the paper, and they have just been read with a simplistic binary stressing, **the time it takes to say each line is the same.** Again: not how humans speak. Variations in pace made by using punctuation actively (the Punctuation Tool), and by varying the lengths of phrasing pauses break the bondage of regular meter and similar line length.

The final trap emerging from the conventional display of verse lines on paper is the sentence trap, and it must be evaded. Since the lines (which are the parts of the sentences) are stacked up like pancakes, and because they've been read with an unvarying dee-DUM meter that takes the same amount of time per line, the actor falls into the trap of assuming that the pause between each of the sentences is the same length. Of course, that's not true! Some sentences connect immediately to the ones that follow, some don't. The space between sentences may hold a major transition of thought or action, or be a reaction to punctuation, like a question mark. Just because the deck is stacked, doesn't mean you have to play along!

Each of the traps adds obstacles to your acting that shouldn't be there at all, because they are artifacts only of printing design and convention, not obstacles presented by content or character, so **break the Molière Traps from the start! Use varied, multileveled stresses, make free use of intonations, and investigate variations of pace through phrasing and punctuation**, among other methods. These are some of the tools you have at your disposal already, and which the Toolkit helps to identify and apply.

ENJAMBED OR END-STOPPED?

Dealing with verse means dealing with verse lines *and* sentences, and they are not the same thing at all. A line of verse, which is usually ten beats or so, *may*be a sentence, or it may not. If it is a sentence, there will be one of three terminal punctuation marks at the end of the line: a period, Q-mark (?), or Ex-point (!). No problem there: it's a sentence, and your job is to understand it and convey that understanding via a strong and committed reading.

But if the line is not a sentence unto itself, then it must be either one of two kinds of verse lines, which are handled in very different ways. An **end-stopped line has punctuation at the end of it,** but it is not terminal punctuation; an end-stopped line will end with a comma, colon, semicolon, dash, or the like, and is part of a sentence, not the sentence itself. It's pretty obvious from the name that there is some kind of a pause at the end of an end-stopped line, used for breathing, for adding persuasive intonation, and to help the actor link individual lines of verse into complete sentences.

The other kind of line is an **enjambed line,** which has **no punctuation at the end of it; there should only be the very smallest of micropauses** at the end, as you flow on to the next line. This is important: **Do not take an extended pause at the end of a line with no punctuation at its end.** Doing so disrupts the energy flow of the sentence as it struggles to pull its parts into a clear and persuasive whole.

Communication and the Need for Tools

[I]n ordinary life one says what one is obliged to, or what one desires to, for a purpose, to accomplish an end, because of necessity or, actually, for the sake of some real, fruitful, pointed verbal action. It even happens rather frequently that when one chatters along without paying much attention to the words, one is still using them for a reason: to pass the time quickly, or to distract the attention and so on.

Constantin Stanislavski[1]

A choice to communicate with someone else requires techniques to do it successfully, and this is as true of theatrical "reality" as it is of our own everyday reality. A person and a character must do the same thing: communicate intentions or needs in a specific way so as to get what they want or do what they must. **The actor's job is to take what *was* written, and transform it into something that *is* being said.** Thus, the actor gives the text, as Shakespeare puts it in *A Midsummer Night's Dream*, "a local habitation, and a name." We turn the past tense of written words into the present tense of action.

Our working text for this project is the dialogue of Shakespeare, and who was better than WS at creating "real" characters? It must be true, then, that both we and his characters use many of the same basic tech-

---

1. Constantin Stanislavski, *Building a Character*, trans. Elizabeth Reynolds Hapgood (New York: Theatre Arts Books, 1936), 105. There are more recent translations of Stanislavski from the Russian (Jean Benedetti's is great), but I'll be using my handy old editions. They do the job, and I know where everything is in them.

niques to put thoughts and feelings into words, and to make them work for us. Stanislavski wrote, "To reproduce feelings you must be able to identify them out of your own experience."[2]

If it's true that when we create and perform, we must use the same tools for communication that we do when "playing" ourselves, then this must be as true for a student's desperate need for a nocturnal burger as it is for Hamlet's meditations upon suicide. We all take a "nuts-and-bolts" approach to communication, and it doesn't matter who the character is, or who you are. **Both real people and virtual people need a toolkit to construct and deliver thoughts.**

THE OVERRIDING IMPORTANCE OF INTENTION

As Stanislavski reminds us at the section's heading, we may speak for a range of reasons, but all those reasons are involved with intentions. **An intention is the motivating desire that lies behind an action, and an action is something done to act out a strategy to achieve an objective or goal.**

For example, you're hungry for a burger. Your objective is to sit down to a nice burger at the diner, but your obstacle is getting to the diner somehow. So your **objective** may be a burger, but your **active intention** is to rouse some burger-producing action from your friend with the car. You need a strategy of linked actions that will move you forward toward your objective.

An intention should be defined clearly, as succinctly and as strongly as possible. It should be a specific action that is doable, not a general feeling or desire that doesn't suggest an action. To help define and clarify your intention in any moment, it's best to use strong verbs, powerful action words that provide you with something specific that you must actually, physically, do. Try to pack it into an infinitive, linking "to" to an action verb, creating an intention that is actable, and that is specific to the situation and need. Here are some actable intentions for our hungry student and the car-owning friend: he needs "to rouse," "to excite," "to entice" his friend into action! Maybe "to coerce," "to challenge," or "to bribe" might do it. The specifics of the strategy come down to the nuts-and-bolts of getting what you need.

---

2. *An Actor Prepares,* trans. Elizabeth Reynolds Hapgood (New York: Theatre Arts, Inc., 1936), 23.

Now, Burger Boy's friend may not be as eager as he is to get a burger late at night. Maybe she's tired, or not that hungry, or it's raining, or she's vegan. Under those **"given circumstances,"** as Stanislavski calls them, "I'm hungry, let's go to the diner," probably won't work. She needs a **stronger motivation** to drive at night, especially for a vegan burger. Knowing all this before you speak, you don't bother with, "Hey, I'm hungry." You say, "I'm *starving!* Let's go to the diner. They've got a vegan burger!" He's refined his intention and strategy in particularly sneaky but specific ways that reflect his strong motivation. He did it by changing vocabulary, using virtual punctuation and intonations, stress levels, and other bells and whistles he feels will communicate—and positively influence—his needs. These are among the nuts-and-bolts of communication.

The student in "The Case of the Nocturnal Burger" wrote and spoke his own dialogue and did both carefully, to gain a greater chance of forwarding his intention and achieving his objective. But when you act Shakespeare's—or anyone else's—work, it is *he*, not you, who's written the dialogue. **Your job is to effectively pretend that it's yours**. According to the basic theory of acting, you *are* the character. So, although you didn't write the words of your role, the techniques you need to achieve an objective using spoken verbal communication, whether inside a play or outside of one, are the same.

The burger saga above reveals that were you the hungry hunter, you'd use certain tools to succeed in making your sentence work for you: you'd choose your words carefully, place emphasis on some words and not on others, use tones or intonations, group some words together into phrases, pause where you want to or need to, contrast ideas against others, etc., and breathe as much as you need to. As an actor, you already know that we work to achieve, as Stanislavski famously taught, **"the illusion of the first time."** So, assume that the intention-charged acts of speech that make up dramatic dialogue, whether naturalistic or Shakespearean, are the actions of a virtual person designed along the same basic lines as you or me: your job is to embody the words to give a voice to the character. Acting teacher and author Robert Benedetti defines acting this way: "Acting is being driven by an urgent and immediate *need* to commit an *action* to achieve an *objective* that will fulfill that need. All external actions on stage need to be *justified* by the inner process of need that causes the external action."[3] [Benedetti's emphasis]

---

3. Robert Benedetti, *The Actor in You* (New York: Pearson/Allyn and Bacon, 2006), 29.

All right, then: What makes Shakespeare's words different from my own? Well, in terms of the intention/objective thing, nothing. But my words here, and yours every day, are prose, or as it is sometimes called, "naturalistic text." Shakespeare's are not; **they have a rhythm and imagery that make his sentences into "heightened text."** Cicely Berry, a masterful voice teacher, defines and distinguishes heightened text from naturalistic:

> I am taking heightened text to mean writing which is built on a rhythmic structure, where there is compression of imagery, and where we understand as much through the logic of the imagery as through the factual reasoning. And I am taking naturalistic writing to be prose, where the structure of the story is built on a logical progression of ideas, where the dialogue is rooted in everyday speech patterns, and where imagery is more incidental than essential.[4]

Shakespeare is the heightened text; your own life, and the plays that try to mirror it, are the naturalistic ones. But remember that we are specifically exploring the connections between the two kinds of language, not their differences. The more you focus on finding and using the connections between heightened and daily language, the sooner the heightened begins to feel and sound natural.

SUPER IMPORTANT! BREATH AND VOWELS!

How does breath relate to thought? What is the relationship of breath—that is, air and breath support for the language—to a creative use of the sentences that make up a role? How does breathing relate to the making of active, intentional speech-acts by the character?

The formula is a simple one: **Thought > Breath > Word.** This is true of your daily speech as well as of the character's. Isn't it true that people in daily life always have however much breath they need in order to complete a thought persuasively? We have enough breath to emphasize what we need to, and enough to intone or extend or manipulate sounds as we want to; we can speak slowly and with clear emphasis or we can choose to be staccato, but no matter what, we simply don't run out of breath under normal circumstances. The thought that requires speaking automatically draws in, and then invests into the words, the breath that those specific, must-be-spoken words require—no more, no less. *So, breathe! It's*

---

4. Cicely Berry, *The Actor and the Text* (London: Virgin Books, 1987), 34.

free! Take as much breath as you need, and take it when you need it! Use breath as your source of vocal power for the character's use. Many young and training actors will rattle on down the lines, not taking any comfortable breaths, until the voice becomes strained and unsupported. Breath is raw material for our art: breathing comes before "acting." Breathe where you need to or want to!

Secondly, vowels. Many excellent acting texts spend pages on them, but if there were a Vowel Tool, it would be this: **only vowels can carry emotion and intonation, and, therefore, intention!** Consonants can't. **Use the vowels actively, holding them for varying lengths as needed to carry persuasive intonations!** That really sums up the use of vowels. Vowels are so fundamental to speech that one expert, Dwight Bolinger, writes, "preliminary to understanding the rhythm of English—and through the rhythm the scheme of accents and the overall shape of utterances—is a grasp of the English vowel system."[5] I certainly recommend following up on this subject in a more expansive work like Cicely Berry's *The Actor and the Text*, which has a full and very useful discussion of vowels.

So:

- **Remember the overriding importance of intention!** Figure out what the character is **trying to do** with the sentence. You always have an intention (however strong or weak) underlying your need to speak a sentence;

- **Remember to breathe and use the vowels!** Breathe as much and where you like, while keeping the drive of the sentence moving forward. And only vowels can carry the emotion and persuasive power of intonation: support the vowels, and use their power to persuade;

- **Remember to avoid the Molière Traps!** The conventions of printed verse can push actors into three traps: mechanical levels of verse stress, similar duration of spoken lines, and no transitional moments between separate thoughts, all because the printed verse looks like a stack of pancakes. Don't fall into the Traps!

- **Remember that there are two basic kinds of blank verse lines** (not sentences; those are usually made up of lines): one kind has punctuation at the end of it (end-stopped), and offers you opportunities to pause, breathe, and use intonations; no punctuation at the end of

---

5. Dwight Bolinger, *Intonation and its Parts: Melody in Spoken English* (Stanford, CA: Stanford University Press, 1986), 37.

a line (enjambed) means you can only take a micropause, and should then move on to the next line. It's in that line where you will find, or make, a place to pause.

Try This . . .

Let's practice breaking the holds of the three traps and connecting lines into sentences through use of the end-of-line punctuation, or the lack of it. These basic skills will make your work with Shakespeare much easier.

Here are two chunks from *King John* (3.1). The first is Constance and the second is King Philip, and just looking at them quickly reveals that they are pretty much opposites in basic construction. Poor Constance; she's been defeated in her dreams of power, and that defeat is trapped in the verse: each line is end-stopped, with different kinds of punctuation. She's pretty desperate, too. The whole speech is one sentence, so have fun: say it out loud, allowing your voice to fill the vowels, use whatever intonations seem right to you to connect the lines into a sentence, and don't forget to breathe!

> O, if thou grant my need,
> Which only lives but by the death of faith,
> That need must needs infer this principle:
> That faith would live again by death of need.
> O, then tread down my need, and faith mounts up;
> Keep my need up, and faith is trodden down.

Here is a small part of a speech by King Philip, partly in response to Constance's speech. But see how the sample mixes enjambed and end-stopped lines; it provides us with a chance to practice connecting the two kinds of lines, **using energy to leap from the enjambed lines to the end-stopped ones, and always working to make the point of each sentence.**

> Good reverend father, make my person yours,
> And tell me how you would bestow yourself.
> This royal hand and mine are newly knit,
> And the conjunction of our inward souls
> Married in league, coupled and linked together
> With all the religious strength of sacred vows;
> The latest breath that gave the sound of words
> Was deep-sworn faith, peace, amity, true love
> Between our kingdoms and our royal selves . . .

And shall these hands, so lately purged of blood,
So newly joined in love, so strong in both,
Unyoke this seizure and this kind re-greet?
Play fast and loose with faith? So jest with God?

Working on both samples allows you to compare Constance's sad, end-stopped lines to Philip's almost leaping ones. These two basic kinds of lines are the building blocks of all of Shakespeare's writing, so play with them enough to feel comfortable with the basic structure. Avoiding the Molière Traps and knowing how to handle the two kinds of lines means that your work will begin in a very strong place.

3

Constantin Stanislavski and the Toolkit

Stanislavski said that the person one is is a thousand times more interesting than the best actor one could become. . . . When the actual courage of the actor is coupled with the lines of the playwright, the illusion of character is created.

David Mamet[1]

Relating Shakespeare's language to your own daily speech is basically using Stanislavski's techniques to understand who the character is, what he or she needs, and why they choose to express those needs as they do in words and in deeds. Which begs the question: **How can I use the naturalistic guidance of Stanislavski to understand how to use the patterned speech of Shakespeare?** The answer is that the two can be overlaid. They work together and inform each other, and some of the ways in which they do are pretty simple and direct.

John Barton, great Shakespearean director and teacher, writes this about the necessary overlay:

> But you may say, "[W]hat's so difficult about acting Shakespeare? What's the problem?" Or indeed, "Is there a problem?" Well, yes, I believe that there is. Two things need to come together and they won't do so without a lot of hard work and much trial and error. First, there's Shakespeare's text written at a particular time for particular actors. . . . Secondly, there are the actors today with their modern

---

1. David Mamet, *True and False: Heresy and Common Sense for the Actor* (New York: Vintage Books, 1997), 21.

habit of mind and their different acting tradition, based on the kind of text they're more used to. . . . How do the two come together?[2]

"Stanislavski" is a name familiar to most in the theatre, but it's his stage name: like Shakespeare and Molière, he was an actor first and foremost. His real name was Konstantin Sergeevich Alekseev. Stanislavski's knowledge came from hard-won experience as an actor and director. **His ideas, usually known as the System, lie at the root of many of today's text-based acting theories.** The System's techniques suggest ways actors can follow toward successful, truthful performances. As each actor chooses her own path, she personalizes the System, creating her own most effective version of it. This is exactly what Stanislavski hoped for; all of the Western acting traditions that are realistically rooted derive from the System, including Method, Meisner, and other variations. Each follows a different signpost toward truthful performance. All are useful, and have their roots in Stanislavski's aim of uniting text, character, and actor through actions. You are free to manipulate the System in any way, as long as it helps you find truth in performance. **And if, as Stanislavski points out, you are a gifted natural actor, you don't need his advice at all!** But, he cautions, you might just as well keep the System around for those inevitable uninspired nights. So as we work with our Tools, we're personalizing Stanislavski's ideas, adding the Toolkit's hints to our own version of the System. Here is an "index card" version of Stanislavski's System useful for using the Toolkit:

Stanislavski's System . . .

- emphasizes emotional truthfulness and physical naturalness in the performance of a role;
- calls for a basic but important skill-set: a relaxed and energized body at the actor's command; a flexible and clear voice with proper support and placement; clear but not affected diction; and a working knowledge of how one's own voice, body, face, and gestures are used to consciously charge verbal communication;
- assumes that characters have a psychology which can be understood by referring to the actor's own emotions, knowledge, or experience;
- requires that the actor understand the "given circumstances," both those that created the character, and those that are specific to the situations the character faces;

---

2. John Barton, *Playing Shakespeare* (London: Butler and Tanner Ltd., 1984), 7–8.

- takes as a given that every action has a strong motivation and an objective; to achieve the objective requires a strategy of linked, specific, actable intentions;

- holds that each character has an essential role to play in the arc of the story, and that there is an arc to each role, just as there is to the entire play: the actor must know both of their character's connections to both arcs;

- and, most importantly to the Toolkit, the System recognizes that the realities of a person and of a dramatic character can be interchanged using something wonderfully named *"If."* It's Stanislavski's term, and his italics; *If* is the core of the imaginative component of acting, asking this simple but heart-felt question: *"If* this were me . . ."

So, to say any sentence in any play meaningfully requires a tiny dose of *If. If* this is my thought, what would I be feeling, and what would I need to do? *If* is often called "Magic If" here, a very American testament to its power; but I think the name robs *If* of its powerful effect. Let's honor this great power with the simpler and more truly magical name: just *If.*

If and the other elements of the System allow us to equate a character with ourselves. Our personal past, our emotions when faced with present or past situations, our reading, the plays and cinema we've seen, our sensitized ability to reference the universal human emotion-and-experience bank—all become tools for *If.* It is the most basic and useful of the Stanislavskian tools. Stanislavski notes that, *"If* acts as a lever to lift us out of the world of actuality into the realm of imagination."[3]

> *If* is the starting point, the given circumstances the development. The one cannot exist without the other, if it is to possess a necessary stimulating quality. However, their functions differ somewhat. *If* gives the push to the dormant imagination, whereas the given circumstances build the basis for *If* itself. And they both, together and separately, help to create an inner stimulus.[4]

Robert Benedetti interprets:

> The *If* allows your "I" to flow naturally into the new "me" of the created character. *If* you live in the world of the character and *if* you

---

3. Stanislavski, *An Actor Prepares*, trans. Elizabeth Reynolds Hapgood (New York: Theatre Arts Books, 1936), 43.
4. Stanislavski, *An Actor Prepares*, 48.

need what the character needs and *if* you do the things the character does to try to satisfy those needs, you naturally start to experience the life of the character and to modify your behavior and thought. This is the same process of give and take that develops your personality in real life.[5]

For Stanislavski, imagination lies at the core of all acting:

This is one of the most important creative faculties. Without imagination there can be no creativeness. A role that has not passed through the sphere of artistic imagination can never become engaging. An actor . . . must know how to create in his imagination a true life out of any given materials . . . [a]n actor is completely free to create his dream . . .[6]

And the root of the imagination, he says, is "nature," by which he means the natural world of objects and persons in which the actor is embedded and within which she or he must operate.[7] As part of the world, the actor, as does each of us, tries to understand the world and how to be effective in it. And the Toolkit assumes that at the core of effectively speaking Shakespeare is . . . speaking! **Understanding your natural, unmediated way of speaking, and imposing that understanding on Shakespeare by using the many tools at your disposal, is the key to overlaying the "two traditions":** psychological acting on the one hand, close analysis of verse and its delivery on the other.

The more an actor has observed and known, the greater his experience, his accumulation of live impressions and memories, the more subtly will he think and feel, and the broader, more varied, and substantial will be the life of his imagination, the deeper his comprehension of facts and events, the clearer his perception of the inner and outer circumstances of the life in the play and in his part. With daily, systematic practice of the imagination on one and the same theme everything that has to do with the proposed circumstances of the play will become habitual in his imaginary life. In turn these habits will become second nature.[8]

5. Benedetti, 29.
6. Stanislavski, *Creating a Role*, trans. Elizabeth Reynolds Hapgood (New York: Theatre Arts Books, 1983), 20.
7. Shakespeare also uses that word, with pretty much the same meaning, as in Hamlet's advice to the players, ". . . the purpose of playing is to hold as 'twere a mirror up to Nature, to show Virtue her feature . . ." When we study ourselves, we study the world.
8. Stanislavski, *Creating a Role*, 40.

Of course, we all exercise our imaginations every day, all of the time. But Stanislavski points out that the imagination is a muscle, in essence: it has to be exercised frequently, specifically trained for its function, or it atrophies. This is most true of actors, playwrights, and other theatrical workers, since we live upon the richness of our imaginations. Imagination is at the core of *If*, and *If* is at the core of acting.

But hand in hand with enriching our imagination, and fueling our desire to keep enriching it, is Stanislavski's attitude toward acting itself. His is a devotional, rather than an egotistical view. The desire to be excellent for artistic, impersonal reasons allows attention to focus on our goal: using our self-knowledge of performance tools, and of human truths, to give well-crafted virtual life to a virtual person. David Mamet, one of our greatest playwrights and a great respecter of Stanislavski, comments:

> Art is an expression of joy and awe. It is not an attempt to share one's virtues and accomplishments with the audience, but an act of selfless spirit. Our effect is not for us to know. It is not in our control. Only our intention is within our control. As we strive to make our intentions pure, devoid of the desire to manipulate, and clear, directed to a concrete, easily stated end, our performances become pure and clear.[9]

When working with Shakespeare, Barton notes that, "I think the most basic thing . . . is the importance of asking the question, 'What is my intention?' If we had to reduce our modern tradition to one single point I think it would be this. It is practical advice which always works and always helps the actor."[10]

We can sum all this up easily, using one of Stanislavski's most famous guidelines: **if you don't do something in life, don't do it on stage.**

When I was a young actor, I was told by my mentor while being directed, "You know, Brian, your knees *do* bend." I was standing, as I apparently often did, with locked knees, either out of bad habit or out of some misdirected or subconscious desire to seem "strong." But, of course, I never did that in real life. And from that moment on, I never did it on stage. If you walk with ease in daily life, why should you stiffen up when on stage? If you speak in daily life with the vibrant tones and inflections of a lively and motivated speaker, why can't your characters? If you don't run out of breath when you speak long thoughts (aka sentences) as a person, why should your characters?

---

9. Mamet, 24.
10. Barton, 9.

So, to sum up a bit:

- our task is to relate theatrical speech to everyday communication so as to find clues for strong choices that personalize your reading;

- we need to use the basics of the Stanislavski System, particularly *If*, to do that;

- we already breathe in a relaxed and natural manner to provide the air needed for vowels, for the open and intoned sounds in speech that carry intention. This must remain as true in performance—or more so—as in life.

In our work, breathing becomes an element of art.

4

The Sentence Tool

Every sentence spoken or written is the expression of a specific
thought: there are no generic sentences. Make the point
of the sentence as strongly and clearly as you can.
At the start, don't worry about meter, lines, or verse—
read the lines together as parts of sentences.

But what is a sentence? According to the *Oxford Dictionary of Current English*, a sentence is, **"A set of words that is complete in itself, conveying a statement, question, exclamation or command."** Even the simple dictionary definition assumes that each sentence is said with some specific intention. In your daily life and under normal circumstances, is it possible for you to speak a sentence that is not individualized and intentional, one that doesn't express a specific need, attitude, or interest appropriate to the moment? One that doesn't seek to define your circumstances? No. No one ever does. Even if you choose to speak a sentence made up of boring commonplaces, that choice is an active one.

Sentences don't have to be long or complicated. Here's a bit of dialogue. You are B.

A: What would you like to eat?
B: Pizza.

"Pizza," in this context, is a sentence, since the questioner will internally add the other words to it, making it, "I want pizza." So there's your complete sentence. Now, to avoid generalities and keep the sentence reading specific, we'd need to determine just how much B wants pizza at that moment. Let's try it this way:

A: What would you like to eat?
B: *(shrugs)* Pizza.

Naturalistic playwrighting can make acting simpler: the shrug structures the reading. But Shakespeare will rarely give you that external stage direction, and that's where Stanislavski and Shakespeare begin to work together.

Clearly, B is not excited by the prospect of eating pizza with A, but why? What's the subtext? Is it because B is bored? Not hungry? Indecisive? Preoccupied? Lazy? Maybe it's even because B doesn't like A very much. We need more *context* to understand the *subtext* of the shrug to give a rooted reading of that immortal line, "Pizza." So B's sentence is more complex than it seems: however short, B's microsentence is "text plus subtext," as is every sentence spoken by you during the day, or performed by you at night.

But there's another way playwrights help us find the thought behind the sentence:

> A: What would you like to eat?
> B: Pizza!

All we really needed to play the sentence actively is that exclamation mark, controlling the level of "excitement" carefully.

Every sentence you speak when you perform from a Shakespearean text must, like the sentences you speak in your own life, be specific, not generic: No generic thought exists. Teachers of acting and directors of theatre always say to their students or their actors, "Don't 'act' generalities! Be specific!" We don't act "sadness": the specific person we are, or are playing, is sad at one moment rather than another and experiencing sadness for specific reasons relating to that moment. We must act the specific character's specific sadness, which always arises out of given circumstances and a very specific context, and Stanislavski makes the point again and again in his first book for the training actor, *An Actor Prepares*:

> Whatever happens on the stage must be for a *purpose* (33);
>
> Don't act "in general," for the sake of action; always act with a purpose (37);
>
> On the stage, there cannot be, under any circumstances, action which is directed immediately at the arousing of a feeling for its own sake. To ignore this rule results only in the most disgusting artificiality. . . . Never seek to be jealous, or make love, or suffer, for its own sake. All such feelings are the result of something that has gone before. Of the thing that goes before you should think as hard as you can. As for the

result, it will produce itself. . . . You must not copy passions or copy
types. You must live the passions. . . . Your acting of them will grow
out of your living in them (38).

Whatever you choose to say or do, or what you guide your character
to say or do, will relate to a specific state or situation, seeking to change it,
understand it, inform people about it, or get them to help. And now we
know that we not only speak sentences: we craft them, we use them, and
actively. We use sentences to frame our thoughts and transmit their content to other minds, where we hope they will do things for us. All sentences are active: that's why experts in the field of communication often
refer to sentences as "speech-acts." "Finding the short chain of ideas, the
series of basic thoughts that make up a speech's argument, is the indis-
pensable first step in an actor's process."[1]

Here are two sentences that serve as excellent examples to explore.
They are the opening lines of *The Merchant of Venice*, spoken by Antonio.
Our purpose here is to turn the heightened text—containing charming
things like antique words, meter, and alliteration (words all starting with
the same sound)—into sentences that make their points. The other stuff
can come later.

> In sooth, I know not why I am so sad.
> It wearies me; you say it wearies you;
> But how I caught it, found it, or came by it,
> What stuff 'tis made of, whereof it is born,
> I am to learn;
> And such a want-wit sadness makes of me,
> That I have much ado to know myself.

The speech is made up of two sentences, each a thought on its own. One
sentence is short, the other longer, and this is something Shakespeare
often does: he balances lengths of sentences against each other. Take a
look at the first two sentences of Hamlet's famous "To be or not to be"
speech and you'll see him use it again.

And, of course, it helps to know that "sooth" means "truth." You
can't express a thought if you don't know what the words that make up
the thought mean. Nor can you if you need but don't have specialized
information about classical references, for example, or Elizabethan terms.
But all of that and more will be in the notes of any variorum. You must

---

1. Barry Edelstein, *Thinking Shakespeare* (New York: Spark Publishing, 2007), 83.

understand what you are saying, or have confidence that you have a grip on the sentence's meaning, in order to make decisions about the most important words of the thought, and how to use the sentence's contents for the advantage of the character. But for these sentences, just a jolt of *If* helps: we've all been where Antonio is.

Read the first sentence out loud (always!) and determine for yourself what it means. Finding the thought inside of the first sentence is not hard. Translated, it's something like, "To tell you the truth, I have no idea why I'm so sad." Now, knowing the thought of the sentence, aware of the point you want to make, say it again with readings that use *If*: what *if* you were Antonio? You've surely felt this way at some point.

We always choose stronger stresses, or tones, for important words that carry information to carry stronger stresses or emphasis, or intonation. The key to saying this sentence, or any sentence powerfully, is to find the **"operative word,"** to use Stanislavski's term. This is the word around which the energy of the sentence gathers: in short, it's the most important word in the sentence. There are likely to be other important words in any sentence, but not *as* important as that operative words. Later, we'll explore the identical nature of Stanislavski's "operative word" concept, and the Elizabethan use of the **"*gravis* accent"** in blank verse composition: it's the most important word or beat in the sentence. There is less distance between Stanislavski/naturalism, and Shakespeare/blank verse, than there may seem to be.

TRY THIS . . .

Play the Sliding Stress game. The strongest stress in this short sentence can slide down the thought, changing the context and specifics of the sentence as it stresses each word in turn. Try it yourself, and see how stressing one beat above the others helps to determine and express the context and the meaning of the thought:

In *sooth*, I know not why I am so sad.

In sooth, I *know* not why I am so sad.

In sooth, I know *not* why I am so sad.

In sooth, I know not *why* I am so sad.

In sooth, I know not why I am so *sad.*

That movement of the operative stress changes the contextual content of the line, and it's all under your easy control. You are the one who chooses—indeed, who *must* choose—that operative word.

The second sentence in the speech has five lines. Obviously, it expands upon the first sentence, and it's easy to see that it is a more complex sentence, but not really any more difficult. For now, read it out loud several times, absorbing its personal meaning to Antonio, but also, using *If*, its personal meaning to you. Expressing *his* emotions, and enacting *his* intentions as truthfully as you would your own is acting.

> It wearies me; you say it wearies you;
> But how I caught it, found it, or came by it,
> What stuff 'tis made of, whereof it is born,
> I am to learn;
> And such a want-wit sadness makes of me,
> That I have much ado to know myself.

Phrases are groups of a few words. They are herded together by punctuation, or by micropauses (more on that later). The first line of the speech above is two phrases, and Shakespeare or his editors have given you lots of nice punctuation to help you connect the bits and pieces into one thought. The punctuation connects, rather than separates, word groups. As such, they usually bring with them some degree of an upward inflection, which helps the connection of the phrases. Downward inflections separate, which makes them good for terminating thoughts, but not for connecting the parts of those thoughts.

Sentence two is a good sentence to work on because it has a lot packed into it, but is easy to understand. "'Tis" is about the only archaic word in it, and that obviously means "it's." Antonio notes the detrimental effects of his depression upon himself and on others; he lists and seems to reject possible modes of origin for his sadness, as well as for its structure and its nature; he goes on to point out his complete ignorance of all of the above and, finally, complains that the weariness of dealing with the depression has drained his wits so much that he doesn't recognize his own behavior. Do you agree that this pretty much pins down the thought behind this seemingly complicated sentence? I say "seemingly" because it isn't really complicated: it's just got more parts to it than a sentence like, "Pizza!" Say it enough times to feel very secure about its meaning. Relax into breathing where needed. Let the punctuation help you to connect the parts and keep it all going with inflections.

A word about keeping energy going through a long sentence: Imagine a small ball bouncing from beat to beat, happily bouncing its way down the sentence. Years ago, there were musical short features along with the main film in movie theatres, and later on, on television. "Follow the bouncing ball!" was the advice of a voiceover, and the ball would bounce from major word to major word to help anyone singing along with the rhythm and the pace.

Take over the job of that little ball. After you've read sentence two, or any sentence, enough times to feel comfortable with its words and content, **imagine the ball bouncing atop your major vocal stresses and most powerful tones as it moves down the lines of the sentence. The bouncing ball can help you visualize pace and rhythm,** as you bounce from important word to important word, or explore changing stress levels by bouncing the ball harder and higher.

You'd be surprised what a bit of creative visualization can do.

TRY THIS . . .

Look at the translation below. It's now presented as prose. Think of it as a speech in a book rather than one in a play. The text, its content, and rhythm stay the same, regardless of its form on paper, but very often, a training actor or an unwary one, will be unhappily influenced and constrained by simple typography (remember the Molière Traps). As we start our work, let's get rid of any hang-ups related to the odd way that heightened text appears on paper. This is the sentence in an everyday transcription—you'll likely find that you feel a bit less controlled by the text when you encounter it this way.

> "In sooth, I know not why I am so sad: It wearies me; you say it wearies you; but how I caught it, found it, or came by it, what stuff 'tis made of, whereof it is born, I am to learn; And such a want-wit sadness makes of me, that I have much ado to know myself."

Using *If*, and your knowledge of what the sentence means to Antonio, keep these things in mind as you work on varied readings of the sentence:

- **breathe:** it's free; take as much as you need, wherever it seems logical;
- use as many levels of stress as you can, choosing to **hit some words much more than others,** guided by what seems important to Antonio as seen through your eyes;

- hit the **verbs with a bit of extra stress**: there are lots of them in the sentence, and that will activate the reading greatly, since they are action words;

- **use the punctuation** to allow breathing, provide intonations connecting the parts of the thought, and keep it moving along as one developing idea;

- **take advantage of the repetitions:** Antonio is using: repetitions of **words** like "it," which appears six times in the sentence (including "'tis"), or repetitions of **form** like "caught it, found it, came by it," or repetitions of **sounds** (called alliteration) like "w," as in "what, whereof, want-wit." These need to sound as though they are not accidental (because they couldn't be), but actively chosen by the character to accomplish an intention through action.

There are certainly lots of methods that each of us, and our theatrical avatars, have at our disposal to personalize the oral reading of a sentence. And using the tools isn't so much about learning new tools as it is about noticing the familiar ones that have always been there, waiting to be used consciously and with purpose.

By now we know that short sentences can pack a real punch ("Pizza!"). And short sentences are great to study as a way to understand the functioning of sentences in general. Here are some simple sentences from *The Merchant of Venice* for you to translate and of which you'll gain command, "making them your own," as the theatre saying goes. I'll note in passing that I have added a comma or a letter in a few places where it doesn't do any damage, but helps you a good deal for this exercise, and the bracketed word is a modern equivalent, so your work can proceed. In these sentences, and many others in Shakespeare's works, you'll run into the good old Elizabethan "doth," which means "does," and is pronounced "duth."

> You were best to tell Antonio what you hear;
> Yet do not suddenly, for it may grieve him.

> Quick, quick, I pray thee; draw the curtain straight [quickly]:
> The Prince of Arragon hath ta'en his oath,
> And comes to his election presently.

> But come at once;
> For the close night doth play the runaway,
> And we are stayed for at Bassanio's feast.

> You take my house when you do take the prop
> That doth sustain my house. You take my life
> When you do take the means whereby I live.

Hard work? Well, not really, so far. But John Barton warned us that it can be very hard work; as your work becomes more sophisticated, it's unavoidable. That's why you should always work from a text with good notes—they'll help you a lot by removing your obstacles to confidence, the confidence that comes from **knowing what you are saying and meaning it.** And remember this above all: everything we're **learning** is actually **revealing**: we're consciously exploring things that you already do when you speak your own sentences every day.

Try This . . .

Here is a sentence from *Julius Caesar*. Cassius is talking to Brutus, trying to persuade him to join in the conspiracy to kill Caesar. I've set it up in verse and prose so you can play with both and discover for yourself that there really isn't very much difference if the actor knows what the thought underneath the sentence is and knows something of the sentence's motivation. If there were notes at the bottom of the page, as in a variorum, one would say that "lief" is pronounced "leef," and the phrase, "I had as lief not be," means "I'd just as soon not be . . ."

> I cannot tell what you or other men
> Think of this life; but for my single self,
> I had as lief not be, as live to be
> In awe of such a thing as I, myself.

> I cannot tell what you or other men may think of this life; but for my
> single self, I had as lief not be, as live to be in awe of such a thing as
> I, myself.

Okay, go for it. Make this sentence your own with confidence and clarity.

5

The Punctuation Tool

Use punctuation consciously and actively for phrasing,
breathing, stressing, pausing, and, very importantly,
intonation. Let the punctuation help you string together the
pieces of the thought. Remember that intonation is the clearest
and most effective way into the minds of an audience.

I was working on the proof of one of my poems all the morning, and
took out a comma. In the afternoon I put it back again.

Oscar Wilde

That's a great Wilde quote, and it immediately illustrates what we're
investigating: the power of punctuation and the ways we can use the
pauses and intonations that follow in punctuation's tracks. But as good as
that quote is, here's a better one for understanding what's at stake when
we play around with punctuation. It's from a great and accessible book
on punctuation called *Comma Sense*:

> One of life's great oddities is how it's filled with things that don't
> seem as if they belong together, yet are inextricably joined. Weddings,
> for instance, and clothes you can barely breathe in. Neckties and hav-
> ing a job. King Kong and Fay Wray. . . . Foremost among things in the
> world that shouldn't go together but do are Understanding Punctua-
> tion and Accruing Personal Power. But it's as true as true gets: If you
> don't understand punctuation, you can't write right. And if you can't
> write right, you can't positively influence so much of what's critical to
> your life.[1]

---

1. Richard Lederer and John Shore, *Comma Sense* (New York: St. Martin's Press, 2005), xi.

Substitute acting for writing: you can't act well if you don't understand how to use the punctuation in your text to your own advantage, because you use complex virtual punctuation as you speak in life. Writing is condensing an idea into a carefully ordered succession of inky squiggles on paper, squiggles of two types: letters and punctuation marks. The squiggles have meanings, and their order and grouping do, as well. **Acting is the art of unfolding the text to reveal the original idea, guided by syntax, circumstance, and commonsense language use.**

So the idea of punctuation relating to your personal power in life is a very important one. Manipulating the punctuated pauses and their intoned vowels, and understanding the relationship of those things to the phrasing of thoughts, leads to varied and energetic readings that are under the actor's control. Acting is driving home thoughts with emphasis, which Stanislavski points out may be achieved by using strong stresses, intonation, or the duration of the vowel, preferably with all three working together.

But there is an essential function of punctuation that works specifically for actors, and headlines the multiple reasons that punctuation is worth taking seriously. As Lynne Truss writes, "For a millennium and a half, punctuation's purpose was to guide actors, chanters and readers-aloud through stretches of manuscript, indicating the pauses, accentuating matters of sense and sound, and leaving syntax to look after itself."[2]

Punctuation guides the actor through the thought, helps to connect parts of thoughts into wholes, and indicates pauses for breathing, for intonation, and for dramatic effect. Punctuation adds essential energy needed by the actor to accomplish the goal of any sentence spoken in a theatre: changing the mind of the audience in some meaningful way.

There are inevitable connections between punctuation, pauses, and intonation. I'm sure you see the logical connections already: the punctuation creates pauses of varying lengths, which are used for things like breathing, of course, but after that, the most important function of punctuated pauses is providing the space into which intonations drop. The punctuation marks pry open parts of the sentence, expanding into the pauses that are now at the actor's disposal as persuasive tools. Earlier in the book, we discussed the importance of breath and vowels: well, **vowels *are* intonations,** and, of course, the tones can only be carried by breath. Always remember that breath is free and no one's counting.

2. Lynn Truss, *Eats, Shoots & Leaves* (London: Profile Books, 2003), 72.

Intonations, the persuasive or explanatory tones we use when we speak, are essential for using language to create dramatic effect. Intonation is, says actor Michael Pennington, **"the shortest possible route between the speaker and the audience, isn't it?** It's a way of communicating. [The actor] has only one opportunity to convey it to an audience whose attention may be difficult to hold. **The inflexion is the clearest and most economical way of doing that."**[3]

So, punctuation in written prose or verse-dialogue is the objectified, visual code of the sounds and pause patterns we use every day when we speak impromptu. And it makes sense that the interpretation and active use of punctuation is just as essential for speaking Shakespeare's words, or the words of a character in a naturalistic play, as it is for you each day. We know that you and Shakespeare use language in basically the same way, although his is "heightened" and yours is "naturalistic." But you always use punctuating pauses, tones, and duration of vowels when you speak. In fact, John Barton notes that there **"is no basic difference between approaching a character when he plays Shakespeare and when he plays any other author, ancient or modern."**[4] Your "spoken punctuation" is virtual, of course, existing as audio tones, and related to pauses in the flow of the words and ideas. When we interpret text theatrically, **we endow to a group of small symbols—dots, lines, curves, and squiggles—the powers of committed breath, of personal energy, and of the intonation that makes our daily language sound real!** Without the same use of activated punctuation in our acting as we use in daily life, the lines will likely sound false.

Lynn Truss, an expert on the use of punctuation, illustrates the need for punctuation in general wonderfully in her little book, *Eats, Shoots & Leaves*:

> Punctuation has been defined many ways. Some grammarians use the analogy of stitching: punctuation as the basting that holds the fabric of language in shape. Another writer tells us that punctuation marks are the traffic signals of language: they tell us to slow down, notice this, take a detour, and stop. . . . But the best of all, I think, is the simple advice given by the style book of a national newspaper: that punctuation is "a courtesy designed to help readers to understand a story without stumbling."[5]

---

3. Quoted in Barton, 57.
4. Barton, 59.
5. Truss, 7.

The title of her book illustrates her point: take out the comma and you have two entirely different thoughts. The title with the comma after "eats" is saying "someone eats something, shoots a gun, and exits." But remove the comma after "eats" and you have "something or someone is enjoying a tasty meal of shoots and leaves." Quite a bit of difference from a single, tiny mark!

There is a famous Zen Buddhist question (they're called koans) used to trigger enlightenment: "What is the sound of one hand clapping?" One of the things I ask my students when we begin working together is, "What is the sound of a semicolon?" Like all of the other punctuation points, you do use semicolons virtually in your speech; you use colons, dashes, hyphens, parentheses and, of course, commas, periods, exclamation points, and question marks. Oral, virtual punctuation is as much a part of what you say spontaneously as are your words and stress patterns. All of them work together to create the foundation of believability.

THE COMMA

The sound of a comma is usually an upward inflection that links parts of a sentence. These parts can be phrases, or small groups of three to five words, or clauses, which are larger groups of words that could, if the writer or speaker wanted, bud off into their own sentences. **The pause created by the comma is the verbal space within which the tone occurs. The pause and the tone are twisted about each other inseparably.** To test this further, say this sentence out loud, using a dose of *If* to make it sound real, and as though you are calling it out to someone upstairs: "I'm going to the store to get bread, milk, aluminum foil, eggs, and a jackhammer." Didn't you use an upward inflection or even a more complex multitoned intonation for each of the commas? The sounds of the comma link the series together. Try the sentence again, but using a downward inflection for each of the commas. Sounds odd, no? At the end of the sentence, at the full-stop moment, a downward inflection makes some sense, as long as every sentence doesn't get one: then it begins to sound unreal, since no variety appears in your readings, and that's not true of people's daily speech. The use of too many downward inflections for punctuation marks that should link, not separate, destroys the energy and flow of the verse. Young actors who aren't comma-friendly often do that.

TRY THIS . . .

Say these comma-friendly sentences out loud as many times as feels necessary to feel sure of the meaning. As you do so, pay attention to what you are doing with the commas.

These are some of the king's lines from *Richard II* (4.1)

> O, for fend it, God,
> That in a Christian climate souls refin'd
> Should show so heinous, black, obscene a deed!
>
> Disorder, horror, fear, and mutiny,
> Shall here inhabit, and this land be call'd
> The field of Golgotha, and dead men's skulls.

Do you hear yourself making upward inflections at the commas? If so, you can probably feel the energy those inflections give the sentence, helping it to drive on. If you read them again with downward inflections, you'll see how disadvantaging that is for the character. And perhaps you noticed in your reading how often you were given a chance to breathe; I hope you took some of them, if not all.

SEMICOLONS AND COLONS

"What is the sound of a semicolon?" When Lynn Truss writes about the semicolon, she, like others of an odd group of people (including me), gets quite excited by them. That their use is largely (very largely) unknown to young actors, yet that they are so powerful and useful to the actor, makes the ignorance ironic. Let's end the ignorance about these powerful tools:

> But colons and semi-colons—well, they are in a different gue, my dear! They give such a lift! Assuming a sentence rises into the air with its capital letter and lands with a soft-ish bump at the full stop, the humble comma can keep the sentence aloft all right, like this, UP, for hours if necessary, UP, like this, UP, sort-of bouncing, and then falling down, and then up it goes again. . . . [B]ut the thermals that benignly waft our sentences to new altitudes—that allow us to coast on air, and loop-the-loop, suspending the laws of gravity—well, they are the colons and semi-colons.[6]

---

6. Truss, 106.

Like commas, which link words or short phrases, semicolons also link groups of words. They are usually independent clauses, which are groups of words that could bud off and become sentences themselves, but don't. But the clauses don't bud off on their own because **Shakespeare wants you to keep in mind that the pieces of the sentence form one thought.** This is one of the many wonderful things about Shakespeare's dialogue: some of his sentences seem so pregnant, so rich, that they could split into lots of smaller ones, and, as Truss points out, each semicolon or colon is a chance to put energy into the sentence anew, necessary to carry a long or complex thought/sentence forward to its conclusion.

So to answer our koan, "What is the sound of a semicolon," we might say "slightly upward," so that the semicolon links, rather than separates, the two thoughts. But there are **colons**, as well: Shakespeare uses them a lot. While the semicolon links smaller, stand-alone thoughts into a more complex sentence, the colon is used to link a complete smaller thought to an incomplete thought, known as a sentence fragment. It's also used to add a list to a sentence. Here are some examples:

> I remember what you said to get: eggs, milk, and bread.

> Here's the key to real estate: location, location, location.

> He made one big mistake that night: showing up.

TRY THIS . . .

When you work on the following piece from Wilbur's translation of Molière's *Tartuffe*, remember that **we use many of our tools simultaneously as we speak,** like stressing, pausing, phrasing, and, of course, virtual punctuation. Right now, our goal is to travel through the monologue in a relaxed way: breathe as much as you would like and at logical places, and keep the energy of the thoughts moving forward by taking full advantage of the punctuation to hold it all together. As Lynn Truss pointed out, the semicolons and colons are wonderful opportunities to keep the thoughts highly energized as you work your way toward the terminal punctuation, by which time you have, we hope, made your point strongly.

The sentences have semicolons, but also commas, colons, Q-marks and good old periods. Your job is to use intonations, pauses, stresses, and every persuasive trick you can think of to keep the lines going as you make your points. Don't forget to use the commas to link, breathe, and slip in an intonation while you are exploring the use of the other marks. The mix, the pattern of pauses and intonations resulting from the free flowing of commas, semicolons, colons, Q-marks and periods creates a complex code of emotional information. As you speak, the diligent little punctuation marks are knitting the thoughts together.

But remember the Molière Traps! You have to avoid them, and this is a chance to practice that. To avoid the **Trap of Meter**, consciously vary the vocal level of stressing, striking the most important words with a very strong stress: go for a variety of stresses, based on the relationship of the words to each other. To avoid the **Trap of Pace,** find a varied pace based on the importance of the words, the strong stressing you choose, and, of course, on the punctuation. Let it work: its pauses and intonations will vary your speed of delivery. And finally, avoid the **Trap of Sentences** by working to understand the transitional thought between each sentence. Some sentences connect with each other over the pause between them, and others stake out new terrain. In either case, the pauses between the sentences will vary. Breathe as much as you like, and don't rush.

> . . . yet for the wise,
> True piety isn't hard to recognize,
> And, happily, these present times provide us
> With bright examples to instruct and guide us.
> Their virtue is acknowledged; who could doubt it?
> But you won't hear them bang the drum about it.
> They're never ostentatious, never vain,
> And their religion's moderate and humane;
> It's not their way to criticize and chide:
> They think censoriousness a mark of pride,
> And therefore, letting others preach and rave,
> They show, by deeds, how Christians should behave.
> They think no evil of the fellow man,
> But judge him as kindly as they can.
> They don't intrigue and wrangle and conspire;
> To lead a good life is their one desire;
> The sinner wakes no rancorous hate in them;
> It's the sin alone which they condemn;
> Nor do they try to show a fiercer zeal
> For Heaven's cause than Heaven itself could feel.[7]

---

7. Wilbur, *Tartuffe*, 191.

Ex-points and Q-marks:

About the good **old handy exclamation point there really isn't must to say except that it has unfortunately been adopted by e-communicants as obligatory for every comment or observation.** In fact, I am told by my students that leaving out gratuitous Ex-points in a text or email indicates a distancing or disfavor from the sender toward the recipient. This has led to the use of anywhere from two to four Ex-points at the end of statements that certainly aren't that exciting. It seems a rather frantic way to communicate something. The meaning and value of the mark has been drowned in prattle.

In "real" writing, the Ex-point, of course, indicates an excited state, and one in which some point is being emphatically made. Of course, they are great for the actor, as they are loaded with energy the character can use. But beware: there should be an Ex-point Molière trap! The energy level of an exclamation point is not set. Just as performing meter requires many levels of stress, and just as varied pauses need to be used carefully and integrated into the flow of the language, so the level of the exclamation point must be carefully chosen; if you have lots of them, one must vary the energy each one gets. And the intensity asked for by an exclamation point doesn't have to be loud to earn its punctuation: the Ex-point is not necessarily about volume. Think of Ex-points as you do meter: assume that the point is capable of many levels of potential vocal support. This will add yet another tool for variability to the actor's kit.

Question marks are a bit of a different story. In today's use of intonations in spoken American English, the Q-mark is often used ambiguously: it is commonly turned from the curling upward inflection of a traditional usage into a downward, terminal tone, turning a question into a statement. Try to avoid that: the mark is there for a reason.

Q-marks have two basic functions: interrogative or rhetorical. In the interrogative, a question is being asked to which an answer is expected. Simple enough. But the rhetorical form asks a question to which an answer is not really expected: the question structure is being used as an aggressive tactic, as sarcasm, or as a way to introduce information without making direct statements. Here are some lines by Clifford in *Henry VI, 3*, illustrating the rhetorical use of the Q-mark. Clifford is confronting Henry on his weakness in political issues:

> My gracious liege, this too much lenity
> And harmful pity must be laid aside.

To whom do lions cast their gentle looks?
Not to the beast that would usurp their den.
Whose hand is that the forest bear doth lick?
Not his that spoils her young before her face.
Who 'scapes the lurking serpent's mortal sting?
Not he that sets his foot upon her back. . . .
Were it not pity that this goodly boy
Should lose his birthright by his father's fault?
And long hereafter say unto his child,
'What my great-grandfather and grandsire got,
My careless father fondly gave away'?

All of those Q-marks are rhetorical.

DASHES, HYPHENS, PARENTHESES, AND ELLIPSES

All of these things work in similar ways, but they are certainly not identical. Dashes and hyphens are often confused, but their uses are quite distinct, and different editions of Shakespeare use dashes and parentheses interchangeably. And ellipses are slippery . . .

Here's what they do in brief, with more about them to follow.

- A dash is involved with interruptions: a speaker self-interrupts when words fail, or she experiences a thought transition, or chooses to use two dashes—one in front and one in back—(like that) to insert an image or subthought into a sentence and get it noticed. The dash is also used by writers when a speaker is interrupted by another speaker.

- A hyphen is used to link smaller words into a new one; almost always, that compound word serves the character's expressive needs in a new and active way. Many of Shakespeare's hyphenated creations have become part of our everyday language.

- Parentheses (plural of parenthesis) interject an image or subthought into a larger sentence, but—unlike the double dash—does so with subtlety, not prominence, so that the parenthetical phrase (as it's called) adds its information or has its effect but doesn't slow down or redirect the sentence's meaning.

- The ellipsis (as in . . .) is used for more things than one would think: it allows a speaker to slow down and pause, once or several times, while clearly intending to pick up the thought again; a speaker can use it to trail off at the end of an uncompleted thought; or it can be used purposefully by a speaker to entice another speaker to pick up the thought. Clearly, intonations matter greatly to the use of ellipses.

TRY THIS . . .

Here are a few of Shakespeare's hyphenated inventions. Try saying the pairs below in both ways as written, giving them some *If*, and see what happens to the stresses and intonations:

want-wit, or want wit

heart-sick, or heart sick

be-all and end-all, or be all and end all

cold-blooded, or cold blooded

fortune-teller, or fortune teller

full-grown, or full grown

high-pitched, or high pitched

marriage-bed, or marriage bed

never-ending, or never ending

new-fallen, or new fallen

snail-paced, or snail paced

well-behaved, or well behaved

wild-goose chase, or wild goose chase

In all of these examples, you can probably hear that you speak/use the words in different ways. The hyphen has a real effect on pace, pauses, and intonation.

It's obvious that punctuation is powerful, offering ideas for pauses and tones that are all tools of persuasion. Take some time to read some of your favorite Shakespeare, perhaps even material familiar to you, but read it for the punctuation. As you work your way through a speech you like, investigate what the marks are suggesting. Try the combinations of possible pauses and tones the marks suggest; you'll see that they really help the work of expressing the point of a sentence honestly.

Actors need to see **punctuation for what it is: a code, one made up of pauses and intonations** that, when actively used by actors as acting choices, can affect the words' meaning very strongly. In fact, **"meaning" is, itself, a code: it's a code of syntax,** of the information in the words themselves.

But there is yet another code at work in blank verse: the code of energy, or what we usually call "meter." The meter is not an obstacle: it's a way to study how energy has been packed into sentences by their author, in what pattern, and how strongly. Knowing how to decode the words and their meaning, how to interpret the code of punctuation, and how to understand the relationship of meter to energy will make your work very strong.

6

The Stress Tool

Shakespeare's work was meant to be spoken using at least three
distinct levels of stress: a light one, a widely ranging middle
stress, and a very strong stress. These are flexible and under
the actor's control. Remember that there can only be one
strongest stress in any sentence. Decide on it and hit it hard:
that will help organize meaning and context.

Shakespeare had this wonderful rhythm which . . . was either for speed or slowness. You learn to go from emphatic word to emphatic word like springboards, and when you want to slow up you lean on them a bit. Once you know about that, it's ordinary talk really, it's life, it's the way we talk. After all, we don't emphasize every word when we talk, do we?

Dame Edith Evans

Metriphobia is my word for the dreaded malady striking those learning to perform Shakespearean and other kinds of classical heightened text: the fear of meter. I think metriphobia grows from a misunderstanding of meter's function, which is to capture in writing the energy pulses of a character's intentions.

Metriphobia confuses and stops many young actors in their naturalistic tracks. "It's artificial," some think. "It limits my freedom as an actor. I can't do it, it's too old, too tough, too antique. You need to be an expert, you need to be British, you need . . ." If you feel any of these uncertainties or all of them, consider these points:

- that in your daily use of English, you already speak rhythmically;
- that the reason iambic pentameter became the standard form for verse drama is its relationship to everyday spoken English;

- that the meter of a line (which, remember, is part of a sentence) is based on the syllables and order of the words making it up;
- that we use multiple levels of stress as tools of emphasis and intonation when we speak, not the five dee-DUMs of mechanically read blank verse. We use at least four or five levels of stress with sliding levels between them.[1]

If these things aren't part of your understanding of how to use meter, then of course you're afraid of it. Without a knowledge of how everyday and natural rhythmic meters are, we're caught in the notion that iambic pentameter is made up of inviolable dee-DUM iambs.

But it's important to realize that stresses are not simply *in* language; they are an aspect of the way we experience language physically. "In reading metrical verse, it is crucial that we feel the beats as we speak: if this happens, there is no need to make a special effort to bring out the meter in our pronunciation."[2]

Another way to look at this is the way Dame Edith does. She points out that it's everyday speech that provides the clue to using what we usually call the levels of stress in metered verse. We don't emphasize every word when we speak; we have reasons for stressing the beats we do, and making sure that they carry more stress than the words of the sentence that supports them.

But Stanislavski himself is the best presenter of the ideas:

> Stresses have varying qualities: strong, not so strong, weak, barely perceptible, short, sharp, light, long, heavy, up-down, down-up, etc. . . .
> The art of the speaker or reader lies in successfully distributing all the degrees of stress throughout the sentence, speech, scene, act, play or role, and putting them in perspective. [3]

The Stress Tool's simplest function is to explode a false notion that the verse is made up of two-beat units of a prescribed weight. With a minimum of three or four levels of stress, the actor has great freedom to speak the character's heart. Why is this needed? Because **the choice of the strongest stress in a sentence is the key decision the actor must make.** It pins down what the actor/character thinks is the point of the sentence.

1. Kenneth Pike, "General Characteristics of Intonation," in *Intonation*, ed. Dwight Bolinger (Middlesex, UK: Penguin, 1972), 84.
2. Derek Attridge, *Poetic Rhythm: An Introduction* (Cambridge, UK: Cambridge University Press, 1995), 64.
3. Constantin Stanislavski, *An Actor's Work*, trans. Jean Benedetti (New York: Routledge, 2008), 454.

We speak in prose, not verse, and we might be tempted to think that it's only metrical writing that reveals a hidden rhythm, but that's not so: much of what we speak or read each day as prose or naturalistic writing has a rhythm. To prove this is pretty easy; examples abound. As a truly random example, I was reading *The Woman in White* by Wilkie Collins recently and was struck by this sentence: "The clouds were wild in the western heaven, and the wind blew chill from the sea." Say it out loud, read it with vigor, use it to create the images the speaker wants to evoke and give yourself an *If* motivation for the speech, and a powerful rhythm emerges.

In fact, even though it's prose, the rhythm is so strong that it can be analyzed metrically and could be the lines of a poem.

> The clouds were wild in the Western heavens,
> And the wind blew chill from the sea.

The first line—one clause of the two that make up the sentence—is a full line of iambic pentameter, with ten beats and minor variations from the regular form, which is the classic and to-be-avoided dee-DUM, dee-DUM. But however minor, exceptions to the regular format is why Shakespeare's kind of verse is called "blank verse." It's flexible enough to carry the full weight of thoughts like Marlowe's, Shakespeare's, and all the rest.

The second clause is another story: that clause is in **iambic tetrameter (eight beats)**: "and the *wind* blew *chill* from the *sea*." It's a common metrical form, and you are very familiar with it, I'd be willing to bet. It's the meter used by Dr. Seuss. It's also common in older folk songs and ballads. Dr. Seuss's tetrameter is rigid and regular. Technically, it's known as "strong-stress" or "isochronic" verse: a pulsing meter with eight beats per line, four strongly stressed. And because it's only eight beats, unlike Shakespeare's ten-beat lines, there really isn't any place in the shorter line to pause, nor a reason to do so. Where are the internal pauses in this? At least there's one internal comma!

> I do not like green eggs and ham,
> I do not like them, Sam-I-Am,
> I do not like them in a car,
> I do not like them near or far . . .

It's only the commas at the line ends that give us any pauses; the lines are too short for internal punctuation or for midline pauses.

On the other hand, a line of blank verse or pentameter, with its ten beats, is long enough to **allow phrasing pauses; it can hold enough into-**

nations to satisfy even Shakespeare; and it can take advantage of the invaluable midline pause, which allows a quick breath, some phrasing, and/or a place to drop in a punctuation mark. There is no major playwright from the Elizabethan or Jacobean periods (the periods of theatre verse that we're concerned with) who regularly used any metrical form other than iambic pentameter. That's why you should not fear meter: within limits, you can manipulate it. Meter is a friend, and not a formula, and should be mined actively for acting choices that help the character communicate needs and accomplish goals.

The stress pattern of verse determines its emotional content and direction. If you know how and why a character stresses what he or she does, you understand the character's needs and intentions. The pulse of the meter is the energy of a virtual person's being, and blank verse seems uniquely suited to carry character energy.

In my sixth-grade experience, the "frame" of iambic verse (the form of a regular line) was pounded into me by Mrs. Sipperley, surely the gold standard of wrong ways to approach Shakespeare: "It's 'dee-DUM, dee-DUM'—repeat three more times! Do that for all the lines!" High school was a bit more sophisticated, what with Mr. Gunter's "Every line has ten beats arranged in pairs of 'lesser-greater' stresses called 'feet,' and there's five feet with ten beats, and they alternate like 'dee-DUM, dee-DUM.'" No wonder we've grown up thinking that iambic pentameter was mechanical and something to be feared. But the meter is, in fact, a verbal oscilloscope, recording both the powerful pulses carrying thought and emotion, and the smaller pulses that sustain those beats or words.

As modern actors, how can we reconcile this seemingly mechanical, structured quality with naturalized performance? Just as your pulse registers the constant flow of life in you, so does the meter, underneath and within the words. The character, and therefore the actor, experiences the need for strong stresses on specific words to be used as tools to carry out intentions. In life and art, we actively and deliberately choose to stress certain beats more strongly than others.

LEVIS, CIRCUMFLEXA, GRAVIS

Poets and theorists of verse in Shakespeare's day, Stanislavski, and modern experts in meter all agree that iambic or blank verse is built upon at least three levels of variable stress, rather than the rigid dee-DUM of Mrs. Sipperley's sixth grade lesson. That there are multiple levels of stress available to the actor, and that blank verse is not a rigidly proscribed scheme, but a flexible one at the actor's command, frees the actor from metriphobia.

So there is no rigid pattern here: meter is simply a way to capture the throb of passion and intention in verbal life, as true for you in life as it is on stage. But even three levels of verbal stress is less than we use in our daily lives. As one analyst puts it baldly, "I assume four levels of easily discernible stress in normal English speech,"[4] and I've even run into an expert who said there were five.

We're directed toward interpreting meter through a minimum of three stress levels by three authorities who approach pentameter from different but complimentary perspectives: **George Gascoigne**, an influence on Shakespeare, who tells us directly that there are three levels used in the English poetry of his time; **Stanislavski,** who focuses on using three levels of stress in analyzing naturalistic dialogue; and **contemporary metrical experts,** who also recognize three levels to stressing.

George Gascoigne was an important early Elizabethan poet whose plays influenced Shakespeare's early career. In 1574, Gascoigne wrote a guidebook on versification for an aristocratic private student, laying out simple but essential rules for verse. And it's a way of looking at verse that's very helpful to actors, who must use *If* to turn virtual written thoughts into their own living ones. Gascoigne writes:

> And in your verses remember to place every word in his natural emphasis or sound, that is to say in such wise, and with such length or shortness, elevation or depression of syllables, as it is commonly pronounced or used: to express the same we have three manner of accents, *gravis, levis,* and *circumflexa,* the which I would English thus, the long accent, the short accent, and that which is indifferent.[5]

Multiple, rather than binary, levels of stress give the actor greater flexibility to express the character's needs. I like Gascoigne's terms for the stress levels: *levis* (levity or laughter), *circumflexa* (tensile and flexible), and *gravis* (grave or weighty). The more familiar contemporary terms (less descriptive and useful, I think) are light, medium, and strong. The concept of "middle" stress doesn't carry with it the tremendous freedom endowed

---

4. Susanne Woods, "The Origins and Art of Versification in Early Modern English," in *Approaches to Teaching Shorter Elizabethan Poetry,* ed. Patrick Cheney and Anne Lake Prescott (New York: MLA, 2000), 79.o.

5. George Gascoigne, "Certain Notes of Instruction Concerning the Making of Verse or Rhyme," in *'The Posies' of George Gascoigne,* ed. John W. Cunliffe (Cambridge, UK: Cambridge University Press, 1907), 467.

by the idea of *circum*-flexing verse: the energy can be anything between "light" and "heavy." The term *"gravis"* conveys much more than the prosaic "heavy." "Heavy" is leaden, the word weighs the idea down, but *"gravis"* indicates gravity, and strong character commitment to forcefully declaring one's meaning. **The *gravis* stress—and there is only one per sentence—organizes the other stresses, as well as determining the context of the thought.** These activated and energized terms for levels of meter avoid the shallow categorization of dee-DUM dee-DUM or even of "light, medium, and heavy."

Gascoigne also points out that a great poet chooses words that carry the meter naturally, though their syllables, thus creating a sense of naturalism when read. It is the bad poet, he says, who stretches the logic of the meter to the breaking point by arranging words that, when spoken, do not sound real or natural but torturously "poetic." Since we can probably agree that Shakespeare is the most "natural" of all writers within the iambic world, **if we use multiple stresses on Shakespeare's arrangement of the lines' syllables,** we will be discovering the living spirit of the character speaking the words.

Stanislavski use a multilevel analysis tool for his naturalistic work, just as Gascoigne does for Elizabethan verse. He calls for a "scale of accentuation: heavy, medium, light. As in painting, where there are strong and light tones, half tones, quarter tones, in colors or chiaroscuro, there is in speech a corresponding gamut of varying degrees of force and accentuation."[6] Stanislavski points out that truthful, "naturalistic" performance requires slides—"half-tones," as he refers to them—and we are reminded of this by the analysts who study speech and who tell us that we use up to five levels of stressing with slides in between. Thus, the two traditions, to use Barton's phrase, can be overlaid in each line of Shakespeare that we say.

Modern metrical investigators like George T. Wright, who has written the only book that deals exclusively with Shakespeare's uses of meter, names the three levels as "in any degree of stress: weak, intermediate, or strong."[7] Wright says that we have no term to describe the "intermediate" level of stress, but of course, as we know, Gascoigne does: *circumflexa*. Being able to "flex" the middle level of stress gives meter its vibrancy. So keep in mind that although we may use the rather bald words "intermedi-

---

6. Constantin Stanislavski, *Building a Character*, trans. Elizabeth Reynolds Hapgood (New York: Theatre Arts Books, 1949), 156.
7. George T. Wright, *Shakespeare's Metrical Art* (Berkeley, CA: California University Press, 1988), 10.

ate" or "medium," those words signify an inherent capacity for flexibility: the medium stress can slide from the upper reaches of "light" to the lower edge of "strong." Rather than being rigid, meter begins to assume almost musical qualities. Wright continues, echoing Gascoigne, **"These variations, commanded by a skillful poet, can go a long way toward making iambic pentameter carry a strong flavor of natural English speech."**

For Stanislavski, the strongest stress goes to the **"operative," "effective," or "key" words,** with medium and varied stresses going to the words that support those key words, and light stresses for the grammatically necessary words like articles ("to," "a," or "the"). He notes that, "Stress is the index finger, marking the most important word in the bar. The selected word contains the heart, the essentials of the subtext. . . . Stress is our third trump card in speech," noting that pauses and intonations are the other two. Remember: the stresses chart the energy pulses of the character at any one time, and the choice of the strongest single stress decides the thought's context. It all comes out in the stresses, and since meter carries thought and emotion arranged as a pattern of verbal stresses, it's the **syllables** that carry the meter: most of the meter will play itself, as you hit the natural stresses of the syllables making up the words. Great verse-drama writers, as Gascoigne teaches, carefully arrange the syllables of the words of the text to carry the stresses of speech in a "naturalistic" way, rather than one that is consciously and sometimes tortuously poetic. By hitting the stressed syllables of multisyllabic words with energetic and varying levels of stress, the meter's basic construction will become more clear. The remaining issue becomes how to handle single-beat words, and the actor has a great deal of freedom for that, and a special tool as well. More on that later.

Meter (the rhythmic patterns of emphasis carried by stressed syllables) and syntax (choice of words) work together in metered text, helped by the code of tones and held vowels from punctuation. *If,* and your own common sense, helps you find that all-important *gravis,* or heaviest stress, in each sentence. **That strongest stress is also known as Stanislavski's "operative word."** There's only one in each sentence, around which all of the other stresses of the sentence are ordered: the *gravis* stress is simply the most strongly hit beat or word in the sentence, and what that word is, is up to you, arising from your work on the sentences you are speaking. It's really that simple.

Here are a few sentences from Molière, in Richard Wilbur's regular iambic and rhymed translation. Read the lines out loud, but read them to understand specifically how the syllables of each line or sentence carries the meter. Explore how cleverly both Molière and Wilbur arrange the syllables to carry an iambic pentameter rhythm. Approached this way, meter is much less intimidating.

> No, all you say I'll readily concede:
> This a low, dishonest age indeed;
> Nothing but trickery prospers nowadays,
> And people ought to mend their shabby ways.
> Yes, man's a beastly creature; but must we then
> Abandon the society of men?
>
> Yes, Madam, if you wish me to remain
> Your true and ardent lover, you must deign
> To give me some more positive assurance.
> All this suspense is quite beyond endurance.

SCORING THE TEXT

Now that we know that we have the freedom endowed by multiple levels of stress, not just "lesser-greater," we can investigate a **process allowing an actor to map the stress pattern that underlies the verse lines,** using a tool Stanislavski called "**scoring.**" The Toolkit version is adapted from his basic idea about the scoring process:

> First, you must choose the key word in the sentence and highlight it by a stress. Then, you must do the same with other highlighted, but less important words. As to the unimportant, unhighlighted words, they are only needed for the general meaning and must fade into the background. *We must discover interrelationships, gradations of strength, qualities of stress among all the highlighted and un-highlighted words and create a perspective in mind, that will give the sentence life and movement.* This harmonious, balanced relationship of different gradations of stress and individual highlighted words is what we mean when we talk of organization. In this way, we create harmony of form and beauty of architecture in a sentence.[8] [Stanislavski's italics]

Here is the simplest method of quickly mapping energy trapped in a sentence. You can use this simple process for prose or verse, for both naturalistic language and for heightened text. The result is a working text that visually represents your personal choices for energy distribution. The strong, and strongest, stresses will be visually distributed throughout

---

8. Constantin Stanislavski, *An Actor's Work*, trans. Jean Benedetti (New York: Routledge, 2008).

the text, allowing the actor to keep the energy of the reading flowing. Performing the text then becomes the process of getting from one strong-and-strongest stress to the next, and connecting them. Because the strong beats are strong for varying reasons—some because they are verbs, some are at the end of the line, some are character choices, and so on—the intonations and stress levels needed will vary naturally, as they do in life. All of that will be visible on the paper, charted out for your investigation.

Below are the bullet points for scoring. After that, there is a chunk of Shakespeare to score: type it out for yourself, in a clear font and 14-point type, and print out a copy to work on. Why? Because the typing out (even better if it is hand-written) uses another part of your brain than the sections used for reading or speaking: the language will be more familiar to you when you work on it vocally. Use this practice for all monologue work for labs or auditions. Having the hard copy allows you to mark as you please, as part of your investigation into the text. The font and size allow you to work from the text easily. If your intent is to memorize it and perform it and for scoring work, it's just much easier to read and work with. For any marking of the text, always work in pencil and not pen, since you want full freedom to change your choices.

- As per the discussion of the Sentence Tool, work on one sentence at a time; read each sentence out loud as you work out its meaning: not only as a collection of words, but also as a motivated speech-act uttered by a specific virtual person; *If* helps you turn that sentence into a motivated speech-act of your own;

- Underline all verbs and proper nouns (that's the Verb and Proper Noun Tool);

- Underline the final strong beat at the end of every line (the End of the Line Tool);

- Using your understanding of the sentence as a strongly motivated utterance, circle the single *gravis*, or heaviest, stress, which is also Stanislavski's operative word. It is the emotional center and high point of the sentence (the Stress Tool);

- Choose and underline the one or two words, or more in a long sentence, that support the power of the operative word; these are important words, but are subservient to that heaviest, *gravis* stress.

So, what do we have? Any sample of scored verse will visually show the actor a staggered pathway of opportunities for powerful stresses.

Try This . . .

Try scoring this chunk of *Merchant*, Portia's large speech from 3.2. Circle verbs, last line-beat, *gravis*, or operative words: just do this, and the pattern on the paper will help you work your way through the text. There are lots of opportunities to find strong stresses: in the first three lines, which make up two sentences, there are seven verbs, three end-of-line strong beats, and two operative words, one in each of the two sentences. That's twelve strong or strongest beats in just three lines! And don't forget: you can use any level of stress you like, from the lightest to the strongest. And always keep in mind: no long pauses at the end of unpunctuated (enjambed) lines! Micropauses only. Use the punctuation, of course, as a guide for pauses and inflections.

> I pray you, tarry. Pause a day or two
> Before you hazard, for in choosing wrong
> I lose your company; therefore, forbear awhile.
> There's something tells me—but it is not love—
> I would not lose you, and, you know yourself,
> That hate councils not in such a quality.
> But, lest you should not understand me well—
> And yet a maiden hath no tongue but thought—
> I would detain you here some month or two
> Before you venture for me. I could teach you
> How to choose right, but then I am foresworn.
> So will I never be; so may you miss me.
> But if you do, you'll make me wish a sin,
> That I had been forsworn.

Could there be a clearer visual chart of a possible metrical journey for the actor? **So, meter is not rigid: meter is an indication of the emotional condition of a character arising from and reacting to a specific situation,** and it is an active tool to support the character's need to communicate: it's not a set of orders. But because it is verse and not prose, the energy of the rhythm is important. Find that *gravis* stress, hit verbs and proper nouns, assign multiple levels of stress, breathe where you want to, carry the energy to the end of the line, and much of your work is effectively done.

Again, the Toolkit offers guidelines, but no commands: you can do as you like, so long as you make sense, get the points across, root your readings in the character's needs and intentions, and keep in mind that Shakespeare wants those varied stresses, helping you by arranging the syllables to take them.

Stanislavski's Stress Tool

*Stanislavski says that there are three specific tools in your kit
for adding energy and personalized meaning to your work:
strong verbal stresses on chosen key words; holding or using
vowels to vary the duration of words and phrases; and/or the
conscious use of persuasive intonation. Ideally, he writes,
stress, duration, and intonation should be used in combination.*

The contemporary actor of Shakespeare has to find a way to combine what John Barton called "the two traditions": the technical necessities of classic metrical material and the requirements of naturalistic acting based in psychology. "We've talked about intentions and of how the verse works and we're beginning to marry the two traditions, Shakespeare and ours. We're beginning to get a balance by finding the language and by making it our own."[1]

You recall that iambic material uses as least three levels of stress with intermediate states between them, rather than the dee-DUM levels of our earlier training or schoolwork. And it was also pointed out that the Elizabethan writers and critics had names for the three levels: *levis* (**light**), *circumflexa* (**medium or flexible**), and *gravis* (**heavy**). Stanislavski echoed this idea, using different terms for the three levels; and the modern metric expert George T. Wright also did, although he noted that we don't have a name for the middle-level of stress in English, even though the Elizabethans clearly did. We decided that "medium" was as good a term as any, but it's very important to keep in mind that the medium level of stress is, indeed, highly flexible, as its Latin name, *circumflexa*, implies: it bends

---

1. Barton, 52.

around, lower or higher, as you wish, filling up the center of the stress spectrum, and linking the light to the heavy.

Let's return for a moment to the idea that **each sentence in English has only one stress that is truly stronger than any other in the sentence.** Of course, that's obvious, really: there's only one "-est" in anything: the strongest, nicest, tallest, fastest. Read through the sentences below, a mixture of everyday and Shakespearean sentences. Can you really say any of the sentences without placing a stress that is stronger than all of the others that make up the thought? Don't forget that the tricky but helpful and flexible middle-stress gives some words a nice jolt of energy, but not the strongest in the sentence.

What are you talking about?

To be, or not to be; that is the question.

I don't want pizza, I want a burger.

I lost my liberty, and they their lives.

Come on, let's get out of here.

Try it yourself. Pick up any book, it doesn't matter what kind. It can be a novel, a work of nonfiction, or Shakespeare. Read any sentence, or series of sentences, with solid *If* commitment, and you'll discover that each sentence has one stress that is stronger than all of the others in the sentence, no matter how flexible and varied the middle-level stress can be.

It's important to be able to distinguish between a high-level middle stress and the one truly strong one. Being able to do that gives you very varied powers and choices for dealing with metrical, or for that matter, naturalistic, dialogue. That's because this truth about stress patterns works for all sentences in English, whether it's our burger-loving friend's desperate plea, or Hamlet's desperate search for the meaning of life and death.

But let's return to Stanislavski, now that we've done some investigating into that magic *gravis* word or syllable in each sentence. He gives a really useful tip with his strong-stress advice: that **there are three ways, or ideally, a combination of them, to add and play that strong stress.** The first is obvious: hit the beat with **more volume.** The second is less obvious: **extend the sound.** The third is to revisit the **tones of voice** that we noted are so important for releasing character energy from sentences, the intonations, which often accompany punctuation. Of course, in this case, they may not: the strong stress may not have any punctuation near it and the intonation is being used to endow strong-stress power itself.

Duration and intonation are more subtle but just as effective as stressing to add emphasis. In naturalistic plays, duration is often handed to us on a platter, as in a line like, "Oh, noooo!" and, of course, such an extension would carry a complex set of tones. Intonation as a way to stress a beat is related to duration: you need to extend a sound, always a vowel, in order to twist it into a new intonation.

Intonation is notably important as an element of using voice to carry forward intentions. In John Barton's Royal Shakespeare Company master classes, actor Michael Pennington, using the term "inflexion," comments, "It's the shortest route between the speaker and the audience, isn't it? It's a way of communicating. The actor . . . has only one opportunity to convey [the language] to an audience whose attention may be difficult to hold. The inflection is the clearest and most economical way of doing that." Fellow actor Lisa Harrow completes the thought: "It carries the thoughts on from the end of one verse-line to the next. By inflecting, you, as it were, keep the ball rolling in the air from line to line."[2]

Stanislavski devotes a good bit of thought to the various ways that strong stresses can work in text. As we've noted in the section of the Phrasing Tool, and just above in our investigation of the singularity of the heaviest stress, he points out that the "most important word stands out most vividly defined in the very foreground of the sound plane,"[3] by which he means the verbal painting, so to speak, created by the many levels of stress and tone. He goes on to ask if the strongest accent comes from above,

> or is it, on the contrary, moving up from below? Is it bearing down heavily or skimming lightly upward with a keen thrust . . . does it fall suddenly and vanish instantly, or linger for comparatively long? Besides, there exists what might be called masculine and feminine accents. The one (the masculine stress) is definite and harsh, like the blow of a hammer an anvil. Such an accent is brief, cut short. The other (the feminine stress) is no less definite in character but it does not end at once, it lasts a little while. As an illustration let us suppose that . . . after you have brought the hammer down on the anvil you immediately draw it back towards yourself along the anvil. . . .[T]hat long drawn out action would be a feminine stress.[4]

---

2. Both quotes are from Barton's *Playing Shakespeare,* in the excellent chapter on "Language and Character."
3. *Building*, 156.
4. Ibid., 157.

And he reminds us again that "accent can be combined with intonation. In this case the latter will color a word with varied shades of feeling: caressing, malicious, ironical, a touch of scorn, respect and so on." He points out that a strong stress can be isolated between two pauses, or by eliminating or reducing stresses on minor words, allowing the strong word to stand out in contrast. His last advice to us on this very useful tool in our Toolkit:

> Among all these stresses and unstressed words it is necessary to establish the inter-relationship, the degree of emphasis, the quality of the accentuation; one must create a tonal plan with the necessary perspective to lend movement and life to a phrase. When we speak of coordination, what we have in mind is the harmonious integration, inter-relationship of degrees of accentuation volume for the purpose of setting forth certain words. This is how we produce a harmonious form, a phrase possessed of architectural beauty.[5]

What a wonderful idea: "a phrase possessed of architectural beauty." The implication, of course, is that the actor carefully structures the stresses, pauses, and tones to "take the shortest route between the actor and the audience." All of this can be done using the tools in the Toolkit when they combine and interact.

To review a bit before we move on, we:

- define the sentence's point, its core of thought, which always carries the character's (or your) intentions;
- these intentions-to-act arise from a collision between a set of "given circumstances" that define the character (or you) within a specific situation;
- these intentions to act, always specific and never general, seek to affect or solve a problem or need created by the encounter of the character (or you) with the situation;
- by using *If*, we place ourselves in that character's position;
- and by choosing and using a rich, varied and character-rooted combination of stresses, pauses and intonations that often relate to simple, external elements like punctuation, we create phrases "possessed of architectural beauty."

---

5. Ibid., 158.

8

The Single Beat Word Tool

*Pairs or strings of monosyllabic, single-beat words provide
opportunities to personalize a line-reading by adding
extra strong stresses to lines, and therefore to sentences.
The choice by the actor of how to use these extra strong stresses
enhances the personalization of the energy that has been
invested by the writer in the meter. Used with the Stress Tool,
the actor can control meter with a great deal of command.*

All the tools we've looked at so far are smaller tools that fold into the "master tool," so to speak: The Sentence Tool. **Everything we're trying to learn and then do is a part of the process of speaking sentences.**

And we know that Shakespeare's verse-drama is metrical, or built upon a specific rhythm. **The rhythm is a pattern of energy pulses,** some very strong, some quite light, and some in the middle, but it's a pretty broad and active middle, covering a wide range of possible energy choices on your part. Stanislavski tells us that strong stress can be conveyed in several ways, and we've noted that there is a relationship between the multiple levels of stress and things like punctuation, pauses, phrasing, and intonations. They all function together in order to make a sentence sound real, and the Single-Beat Word Tool is powerful: using it, the actor can strongly influence and personalize the energy flow coded into the syllables and beats of the meter. By adding strong stresses (where appropriate) to single beat words that are not already in a stressed position, and regardless of their position in the old dee-DUM, dee-DUM, strength is added to the reading, and more emotional content is liberated.

And you make the choice! That's why this is such a powerful tool in an actor's kit. **Where there are two or more monosyllabic words in a** line, the amount of energy you pump in by adding strong stresses to the otherwise formulaic dee-DUM is up to you . . . or rather, the character. It's the actor's power to bend and flex the iambic frame more to our will.

Try This . . .

Here are some sentences with single-beat words. How many different readings can you supply, shifting around a pattern and a number of strong stresses that you choose to place on single-beat words? Remember that stresses can be carried via the verbal energy of the strike, by the duration of the beats, by their intonation, or most likely a combination of the three.

The first sentence starts with a line that has nine single-beat words in a row; the next line has only one, but with five two-beat words. Notice that all of those final four bisyllabic words reverse the normal stress pattern of the iambic/blank verse, turning the expected four dee-DUMs into four DEE-dums in a row! Of course, Shakespeare is doing this on purpose. As you explore reading the sentence with *If*, add strong stresses to the nine single-beat words of line one; and feel how the punch and power of line two is increased by Will's reversing the positions of the strongly stressed beats of four words in a row. You will hear yourself taking powerful possession of the line through stresses that are clearly part of the character's need to express his frustration. From *H6, 2* (4.1):

> O, that I were a god, to shoot forth thunder
> Upon these paltry, servile, abject drudges!

And another to play around with: nine of the ten beats of this one-line sentence are single-beat words, ready for your stress manipulation.

> Ay, but my deeds will stay thy fury soon.

Finally, here's a beauty! Four lines, thirty-two words, with twenty-eight of them single-beat words: what an opportunity to explore adding strong stresses that are purely from character necessity, and not from the frame of the verse.

> . . . No, rather let my head
> Stoop to the block than these knees bow to any
> Save to the God of Heaven and my King . . .
> More can I bear than you dare execute.

Do you feel less metriphobic about all this as you come to see what power you have as an actor to take control of the character's thoughts? I hope so: the less fear we have of structured language, the more power we have over it. As Sonia Moore, one of the great modern Stanislavski teachers points out, "Rhythm expresses inner experience, and control over it is one of the conditions for mastering the inner technique. Overcoming obstacles on the way to your objective should be of tremendous help in changing the tempo-rhythm."[1]

So the presence of single-beat (or monosyllabic) words provides us with a real flexibility. Since they don't have to obey a required pattern of stresses, we're much freer to choose how we stress them, and this gives us a very useful tool for taking possession of the sentences through *If*. John Barton asks, "So how does blank verse actually work? . . . Its normal rhythm goes 'de dum de dum de dum de dum de dum,' but actually that often isn't true. It sometimes does, but perhaps more often it doesn't."[2]

---

1. Sonia Moore, *Stanislavski Revealed* (New York: Applause Theatre Books, 1968), 41.
2. Barton, 27.

Verb and Proper Noun Tool

Hit verbs (action words) and capitalized nouns (people, places,
or things known to the character) with a strong stress.
This creates the illusion of the character's world of action
and of personal connections or imagery, and adds
strong stresses to help energize readings.

The Verb and Proper Noun Tool is a simple way to investigate where some strong stresses can logically go. The basic idea is that the character knows the people or the places he or she is mentioning, and is mentioning them for a reason: adding stress to the name ties the person mentioned to the person speaking. Verbs operate in the same manner: verbs are action words, words for things the character does, or reacts to. Since they are, as Hamlet puts it, "actions that a man might play," hitting the verbs adds energy to the line. **If you hit the names and verbs strongly when you deliver the lines, they will sound rooted in the life of the character.**

Here is a rousing speech by the Earl of Gloucester in *Henry the Sixth, Part Two,* 1.1. Read it out loud a few times. As you become more familiar with it and get the points of the sentences (which are pretty obvious), give it a strong reading, hitting every name and every verb with more vocal energy, clearly audible, than words you decide are supportive in function, as Stanislavski asks. For ease, I've made bold all verbs, names, and end-of-line strong beats. Note how hitting the names makes you sound like part of that group, and notice how hitting the verbs expresses a range of the character's emotion. Don't forget that you should investigate intonation and duration as tools to add stress. Use all of these chances to charge the speech with energy, and you'll see how varied it will sound, rather than being the rigid force we may think "iambic pentameter" can be.

And there's one thing you have to do: **locate the operative word, the** *gravis,* **or heaviest single stress, in each sentence.** That will be the word around which the thought congeals.

> Brave peers of **England**, pillars of the **state**,
> To you **Duke Humphrey** must **unload** his **grief**,
> Your grief, the common grief of all the **land**.
> **What!** Did my brother **Henry** spend his **youth**,
> His valour, coin and people, in the **wars**? . . .
> And did my brother **Bedford** toil his **wits**,
> To **keep** by policy what **Henry got?**
> Have you yourselves, **Somerset, Buckingham**,
> Brave **York, Salisbury**, and victorious **Warwick**,
> Received deep scars in **France** and **Normandy?**
> Or hath mine uncle **Beaufort** and **myself**,
> With all the learned council of the **realm**,
> **Studied** so long, **sat** in the council-**house**
> Early and late, **debating** to and **fro**
> How **France** and **Frenchmen** might be **kept** in **awe**,
> And had his **Highness** in his **infancy**
> **Crowned** in **Paris** in despite of **foes?**
> And shall these labours and these honors **die?**
> Shall **Henry's** conquest, **Bedford's vigilance**,
> Your deeds of war and all our council **die?**

The strongly stressed names and verbs add lots of energy to the speech, and of course, in addition to these formal elements are the strong and *circumflexa* stresses you choose as operative words for the character. Look at the paper and you'll see a remarkable and useful diagram of stresses arranged on the paper. Go ahead and mark your character stresses, and say it again a few times, exploring how varying those strong stresses in level, and the use of intonations, can make the reading even more personal. **The more active and consciously applied your choices of emphasis, the more personally real the dialogue sounds, especially if there are lots of verbs, names, and ends of line.**

Every sentence has at least one verb, as you no doubt know: without one, you don't have a sentence, all of which contain a verb and a subject (the noun). Some sentences have more than one verb, and as you can imagine or easily prove for yourself, a sentence with lots of verbs describes or represents lots of action.

If you've done the verb underlining and oral reading, it's pretty clear how stressing the verbs in the sample helps to bring the reading alive, because verbs in metrical drama stress the will of the speaker. Put strong stress on the verb when you speak it and you'll *hear* the trapped, personalized power of your reading. Shakespeare helps us in another way, which we'll examine later on: he often places verbs as the last word of a line. One of the tools, the End of the Line Tool, investigates this, so we'll return to the interesting things that happen at the end of a line later on.

But what about the proper nouns? We saw in that extended sample above that stressing the proper names of people, cities, and countries adds a lot of personalized power to the reading. Here's another example that uses names a lot. Try reading it out loud, putting extra stress on the names and verbs, on the end-of-line beat, and with the strongest beat of all falling on the *gravis* word you choose and therefore circle.

Before you read your final scored version, just read the text: look how many opportunities you have for varied levels of strong stresses to personalize the material! Listen to the way the pattern of strong stresses lifts the lines up into the air, making them sound like the specific thoughts of a specific person in one specific situation. As for all of the other words that are not underlined, and that support the heavier words, remember that the normally stressed syllables of the words will take care of themselves, and, when read energetically, will carry most of the meter for you.

From *Henry VI, 2* these are the words of the Captain, who appears only once in the play, to speak a fantastic speech to Suffolk in 4.1, of which this is a part:

> By devilish policy are thou grown great,
> And, like ambitious **Sylla,** overgorged
> With gobbets of thy mother's bleeding heart.
> By thee **Anjou** and **Maine** were sold to **France,**
> The false revolting **Normans** thorough thee
> Disdain to call us lord, and **Picardy**
> Hath slain their governors, surprised our forts,
> And sent the ragged soldiers wounded home.

The proper noun stress is such a useful tool! If you read this sample and add your extra stresses on proper nouns, verbs, and the end-of-line beat, doesn't it sound like the words of a *specific* person, that one man who has this specific information and opinion? **Or to be honest, doesn't it sound like you know what you are saying?** Without stronger stresses on the names, the speech sounds weak and general, and those are enemies to our work. Do you know at this moment who Sylla was? If not, I'd look at the bottom of the page in the noted edition I would be using; remember that we always need to use one of those, and for just this reason. But that's the value of the tool: even if I don't have the vaguest idea who Sylla is, if I really stress the name, lo and behold, it sounds as if I do, because, otherwise, why would I choose to use it in a sentence?

Here are a few mundane examples of everyday speech. Do you hear the proper nouns getting strong stress?

> Let's go to Burger King for dinner.
>
> It wasn't Mary who said that, it was John.
>
> In London, I'll see the Crown Jewels.
>
> *Citizen Kane* is a great movie.

It really works, and it's very useful for making other people's words sound like your own.

TRY THIS . . .

Before moving on, **find and underline the verbs and proper nouns in this speech,** and as a good habit, **the last strong beat of the line.** For each sentence, find your **operative word/*gravis* stress.** In multiple readings, experiment with hitting those chosen words with several levels of varying stresses. Think of it as pattern-forming: look at your marked, scored text, and you'll visually see the clear pattern. And remember: use the punctuation for breathing, pauses, and intonations. And notice how many end-stopped lines, versus enjambed lines, the sample has: this tells you something about the speed of delivery and the deliberate way that Antony is speaking. This is Antony's speech to the crowd from *Julius Caesar*, 3.1.

> If you have tears, prepare to shed them now.
> You all do know this mantle: I remember
> The first time ever Caesar put it on;
> 'Twas on a summer's evening in his tent,
> That day he overcame the Nervii.
> Look, in this place ran Cassius' dagger through:
> See what a rent the envious Casca made:
> Through this, the well-beloved Brutus stabbed;
> And as he plucked his cursed steel away,

Mark how the blood of Caesar followed it,
As rushing out of doors to be resolved
If Brutus so unkindly knocked, or no;
For Brutus, as you know, was Caesar's angel:
Judge, O you gods, how dearly Caesar loved him!

10

The Antithesis Tool

An antithesis is a juxtaposing of two words, images, phrases,
or ideas connected by a word like "and," "but," and
some others. Shakespeare uses them a great deal:
find them, and play them strongly and deliberately,
as an active choice made by the character, usually by
adding stronger stress to the second of the pair.

An antithesis can be very simple, or more complex. See? That wasn't hard. That first sentence is, of course, an antithesis. Antitheses (plural) are elements of our personal, persuasive speech, and they appear very frequently in Shakespeare's work. They appear so frequently that **Shakespeare is often referred to as an antithetical writer.** "This is really most important to come to terms with, for the writing is based on the extensive use of antithesis."[1] He seems to specialize in them, and that's why this tool is so useful. Some are simple equations based upon a "this, *or* that," or "this, *but* that," or "this, *not* that." Others are more complex, with many lines devoted to the contrast. And try this: if you switch the position of "simple" and "complex" in the first sentence, it doesn't change the reading: the second one still gets the extra stress. It's the nature of the antithesis, and how it is said in everyday speech.

I would be less than honest if I didn't point out that some experts, like Patsy Rodenburg, disagree with the basic concept of stressing the second element of the antithesis. She says that "there are . . . problems for the actor who attaches primarily to one side of the antithesis or the other. . . . This one-sided approach entirely misses the point . . . you need to swing

---

1. Cicely Berry, *The Actor and the Text* (New York: Applause Books, 1992), 90.

between the opposites and be on them as you swing."[2] Certainly, since the antithetical thoughts or image/objects come in linked pairs, one will need to "swing back and forth" based on individual cases. But in my own experience, and probably yours as well, there is some extra emphasis, however little the difference, between the initial and the resolving parts of the antithesis. "I like you, but I love her." Can you say that without adding energy to "her" to make the point? What happens if you don't? Like and love can also be antithetical, and that pairing would also likely as not take the stress on the second object. "I may have messed up, but you really messed up." "Really" gets the stress: "really" is more definitive than "may have," and completes the comparison. But let's say this: as a tool to guide the actor, the Antithesis Tool and its essential guidance is empowering to the actor, and a great way to command the language and get full use of it.

TRY THIS . . .

Let's take a look at a piece of Shakespeare packed tightly with antitheses. It's one of the *Sonnets*, 75, and the whole thing is built out of them. The antitheses are italicized. For all of the antitheses in the sonnet below, try hitting the second one a bit harder, with varying emphasis, duration, or intonation (or all three, says Stanislavski), and you will be able to hear the antitheses at work. Note that an antithesis can lead to another one, or even a chain of them: clearly, those are internally connected, as well as being connected by their general form. Remember to use a variorum edition with bottom-of-page notes in the future. With this you'll learn that "twixt" means between, "anon" means soon, "filching" means stealing, "starved" is pronounced "STAR-ved," "pine" means (in this context) do without, "surfeit" means to be stuffed, and "gluttoning" means eating everything in sight. Now there are no verbal obstacles to your work.

Read it out loud softly a few times, letting the patterns appear and connect. Don't forget the very important use of intonations—vowels with tones—as a way to not only handle the specific antithesis at hand, but also as a way of linking the antitheses together to create the arc of unity within the poem. Remember, all the images are related to wealth of one kind or another, and they are linked together by punctuation and the pattern of strong stresses. Try the Tool, and make the most sense out of it that you can. Note that there is clearly a sense of humor working here: can you

2. Rodenburg, 122.

sense it? The angst involved in the relationship of a miser to his wealth and his fear of theft is humorous, especially when compared to the true treasure of the poet's love and his fear of losing it. That sense of humor should be something you search for and find: several of the antitheses contain implicit humor, which then fades into a meditative state for the last quatrain (four lines) and a wistful sadness in the couplet. All of these emotional states are carried as information by the natural function of antitheses and by the character-specific use of them. It's Sonnet 75.

> So are **you to my thoughts** as **food to life,**
> Or as sweet seasoned showers to the ground;
> And for the **peace** of you I hold such **strife**
> As 'twixt a miser and his wealth is found:
>
> Now **proud** as an **enjoyer,** and anon
> **Doubting** the filching age **will steal** his treasure;
> Now counting **best** to be with **you alone,**
> Then **bettered** that the world **may see my pleasure;**
>
> Sometimes **all full with feasting** on your sight,
> And by and by **clean starved for a look,**
> **Possessing** or **pursuing** no delight
> Save what is **had,** or must **from you be took.**
>
> Thus do **I pine** and **surfeit** day by day,
> Or **gluttoning on all**, or **all away.**

Back and forth between two opposites goes the stress, like badminton. And notice something else: **the whole sonnet is only two sentences.** The antitheses and their back-and-forth rhythm keep the sonnet moving forward step by step, and this sample is a great one for working on sustaining the thought throughout the line, and for playing about with end-stopped lines and how they connect to form the developing thought.

But no look at antithesis is complete without the single most famous line in all of English drama, which is also a simple and classic antithesis. Say it out loud and you will hear yourself naturally add more stress to the second of Hamlet's options, likely on the word "not":

> **To be** or *not to be;* that is the question.

The line would be lifeless without that greater stress on the second choice. The next sentence, made up of four lines, is an excellent example of a more complex antithesis expanding on the thought behind "to be."

> Whether 'tis nobler in the mind **to suffer**
> The slings and arrows of outrageous fortune,
> Or to **take arms** against a sea of troubles
> And by **opposing, end** them?

Note that he is using four verbs in this sentence. Every sentence needs at least one verb, but this sentence has four, and four of them are in the second pair of lines (suffer, take, oppose, end). **We know the Tool for verbs: that's another reason to give the second half of the antithesis more stress than the first.** It also gives an actor opportunities for punchier readings than the usual funereal ones the lines seem to invoke: the verbs beg for strong stresses.

Both of these famous Hamlet antitheses use the familiar "or" hinge between the halves of the pair. "But" is also frequently used, as in this example from *H6, 2* (3.2). Suffolk is speaking to his illicit love, Queen Margaret. It's quite intricate, balancing "depart from" against "cannot live," "thy sight" from "thy lap," and "die" against "slumber." Try saying the lines out loud, following this second-stressing idea; take the pauses needed at the punctuation and say it with energy, and you will hear the reading come together:

> If I **depart** from **thee**, I cannot **live**;
> And in **thy sight** to **die**, what were it else
> But like a pleasant **slumber** in **thy lap?**

TRY THIS . . .

We looked at some of the lines from the following speech—Clifford from *H6, 3*, (1, 2)—as a way to play around with Q-marks, but it's a great speech to work on for other reasons, like practicing end-stopped lines, or playing about with a tall stack of short sentences that connect into a larger, overarching structure of thought and avoiding the Trap of Sentences along the way. It's gender-neutral, so everyone can work on it and even use it for auditions.

Every sentence is one half of an antithesis. The pairs of sentences match each other in a driving and regular iambic rhythm. The first line of each pair is end-stopped: it has punctuation to provide energy and intonation to power you on to the second, antithetical thought, and that punctuation in each case is a rhetorical question mark, a mark with a pronounced intonation that acts as the link between the antithetical sentences. The second thought ends with a period, since it is making the point of the antithetical thought. It's likely that your natural tendency while reading this one out loud will be to stress the second sentence, either by emphasis, duration, tone, or some combination of these elements. This is because it makes the point of the antithesis.

But in addition to being a great speech for exploring antitheses, punctuation, connection, and thought-building, it's also a test of your ability to **avoid the Molière Traps** of meter and line duration. Use all of your tools to avoid the traps by deliberately breaking out of them: use multiple levels of stress to avoid the Meter Trap and use pauses, phrasing, and tones of punctuation to vary the length of the line readings to avoid the Pace Trap. Take all the breath you need, in pauses you choose to take, based on punctuation, phrasing, and your strong desire to get the points of the sentences across. Remember to put some extra stress on verbs, capitalized names, and the final strong beat of the line.

The overall intention of the speech is to energize King Henry into opposing rather than accommodating his enemy, the Duke of York:

> My gracious liege, this too much lenity
> And harmful pity must be laid aside.
> To whom do lions cast their gentle looks?
> Not to the beast that would usurp their den.
> Whose hand is that the forest bear doth lick?
> Not his that spoils her young before her face.
> Who 'scapes the lurking serpent's mortal sting?
> Not he that sets his foot upon her back.
> The smallest worm will turn, being trodden on,
> And doves will peck in safeguard of their brood.
> Ambitious York doth level at thy crown,
> Thou smiling while, did knit his angry brows;
> He, but a duke, would have his son a king,
> And raise his issue like a loving sire;
> Thou, being a king, blest with a goodly son,
> Didst yield consent to disinherit him,
> Which argued thee a most unloving father.
> Were it not pity that this goodly boy
> Should lose his birthright by his father's fault?
> And long hereafter say unto his child,
> 'What my great-grandfather and grandsire got,
> My careless father fondly gave away?'
> Ah, what a shame were this. Look on the boy,

> And let his manly face, which promiseth
> Successful fortune, steel thy melting heart
> To hold thine own and leave thine own with him.

The repetition of "not" adds energy to the second of each of the line-pairs, and the point of the antitheses is very clear when the opposition of the images has been made. The example is all the more powerful because, in addition to the images and ideas being contrasted, powerful verbs are as well: "cast" versus "usurp," "lick" versus "spoils," and "scapes" (escapes) versus "sets." He's (Shakespeare and Clifford) also using alliteration, or the repetition of the same sounds, to heighten the energy: "usurp," "spoils," "scapes" and "sets," and the hard K-sound of "lick" and "back." So we have pairs of powerful, short, end-stopped lines, each pair of which is a full sentence and repeats a formula: repetition of the barked monosyllabic "not," multiple verbs, and alliteration of harsh consonants. Shakespeare is concentrating a lot of energy into this set of antitheses.

TRY THIS . . .

Here is another example, and this time, the whole speech is built upon images and things that balance against each other and interlock in complex ways. Not only is this sample a good illustration of the power of antitheses, it's also useful to illustrate how all of our tools work together. This is part of a speech by Northumberland in 1.1 of *Henry IV, 2*:

> In poison there is physic; and this news,
> Having been well, that would have made me sick,
> Being sick, have in some measure made me well:
> And as the wretch, whose fever-weaken'd joints,
> Like strengthless hinges, buckle under life . . .
> . . . even so my limbs,
> Weaken'd with grief, now being enraged with grief,
> Are thrice themselves.

In fact, this eight-line sentence is a tapestry of antitheses. All of the things that make up the sentence—vocabulary, juxtapositions of words and ideas, phrases and clauses, punctuation—are used as tools to express a single, unified thought. As with any long sentence, we need to know what that thought is and we need to investigate how we might best use our tools of stresses, pauses, and intonation to turn a written sentence into the believable, verbal expression of a freshly minted thought.

After the two-line antithesis, the sentence expands into one of six lines, describing how circumstances that rob one person of strength can charge up another. This complex antithesis includes an image chain, linking "joints" to "hinges" and "hinges" to the thing containing the hinge, the arm. It also features lots of verbs, and we've learned how strong verbs can be. It uses alliteration for both verbs and nouns, as in "break" and "buckle," "fever" and "fire." There's repetition: the same word, "grief," is used to contrast the opposing processes of weakening and enraging. Finally, the six-line antithesis is welded to the two-line antithesis by juxtaposing the "well" and "sick" of lines two and three with the broken-hinged, fever-weakened arms versus the energy-charged arms of lines seven, eight, and nine. This is a tough one, because the imagery, which is strong, is also very extended, covering lots of beats and phrases, commas throwing phrases up into the air like tennis balls about to be served.

Earlier in the scene, Shakespeare gives Northumberland an antithesis that is densely compact and one of the most interesting in all of the plays. He hears that his son, Hotspur, has been killed in single combat by Prince Hal, later to be Henry V, and says of his son, **"Of Hotspur, Coldspur?"** In addition be being a dynamite antithesis as compact as an atom, it also illustrates Shakespeare's love of puns, as well as the dark humor that pervades many of Shakespeare's moments of tension. If you just say this phrase out loud right now, you'll hear the natural stress on the first beat of the second name. That's The Antithesis Tool at work, and illustrates once again that underlying strong dramatic readings are the natural tricks of our own communication.

Performing Shakespeare is, as John Barton reminded us, hard work, but it is not as complex a task as it has been made to seem. Learning to speak Shakespeare should be seen as the acquisition of a set of skills and tools, not as mystical hidden knowledge known only to a few.

The next two tools operate very closely with each other, so it's best to handle them together.

The Pause Tool

There are three lengths of pauses in verse drama that are used for different purposes. As you work, consciously observe how tiny micropauses for phrasing; longer, intoned pauses associated with punctuation; and the filled, transitional pauses between sentences, can be active parts of your toolkit.

The Phrasing and Midline Break Tool

English speakers naturally tend to speak in three- to five-word phrases. Micropauses link the phrases into thoughts: without that phrasing pattern, spoken material sounds memorized. A special phrasing pause occurring in the middle of a verse line—usually after the fourth, fifth or sixth beat—is called the midline break. It was put there by Shakespeare to allow a ten-beat line to be handled as two phrases.

A discussion of the power of pauses, be they ever so tiny, involves a very close relationship between the nature of pauses and their variety, and the specific uses with which the tiniest of them, micropauses, are tasked.

"Silence betokens," writes Robert Bolt in his wonderful play, *A Man for All Seasons.* Pauses in the flow of sound are essential for communication of any kind, real or artistic. The words of the **text** carry syntactic information, and **meter** charts the character's investments of energy in specific words or images; but **silences**—some of them an iota of breath, others lasting for long and emotionally grueling moments—are the spaces within which stresses can vibrate, within which punctuation's intonations find a home, and through which the syntax and the emotional throb of the meter can be organized and arranged for maximum advantage by the character. The resonance of varied silences, interspersed as they are along a line of varied sounds, creates a digital code of ones and zeroes: **verbal communication is made through manipulating sounds and silences.**

It's no surprise that Aristotle, in his essential work on drama and theatre, the *Poetics*, places two structural elements at the very core of any theatrical action: *opsis* and *melopoesis*. Opsis, as in optical, means everything seen; melopoesis, as in melody, is everything heard. And that is why silence betokens: silence, the yin to sound's yang, is not an emptiness, but a choice made by the actor to hold up the flow of sound, or to direct its parts for his or her own use. The pauses create a crafted reality that is artistically accepted as a 'true' reality, or at least its reflection. We compliment acting by saying it has verisimilitude, meaning "a similarity or likeness to truth." And that is the paradox of acting: we need to study the pause, to take it apart, in order to use it in performance exactly as we would use it in life. Acting is believable only if, as Shakespeare put it, it mirrors life's daily "commerce of the senses." **An actor's understanding of pause power is a tool for reinforcing the likeness to truth.** As an expert in pause patterns in Elizabethan drama noted, "Although it will become apparent that even in pause patterning there can be much deliberation . . . the total of the patterns is likely to reveal much over which the person concerned has little or no control, almost as people are unable to control their cardiograms."[1]

Like stressing patterns and the musical score of persuasive intonations, the pause pattern of freely flowing speech reveals character information: anxiety, intensity, pace of thought, and more. And of all the elements an actor must engage with in order to perform, it is the character's pause pattern that controls that flowing, living process whereby breath, intonation, connections, oppositions, and tensions are controlled and channeled. If using varying levels of stress purposefully in any spoken sentence releases character energy, then the more energy released, the more likely it will be that pauses of varying types will be needed to keep

---

1. Ants Oras, *Pause Patterns in Elizabethan and Jacobean Drama*, Univ. of Florida Monographs, HUMANITIES No. 3, Winter 1960 (Gainesville, FL: University of Florida Press), 2.

the power of the lines flowing forward. The levels of stress making up the energy text should be as highly varied as they are in your own speech, and the pauses helping to connect and organize the text need to be as varied in length and placement as are the powerful strikes of the meter. The result is truly a "scoring" of the text, bringing out musical elements of rhythm, of phrasing, of a vibrant array of strikes and tones, all resonating within the spaces of the pauses. To fail to do this is to leave oneself open to the Molière Traps: the lack of varied metrical strikes makes the work rigid and inflexible; the absences of pauses and phrasing results in a standardized pace for the line readings; and the ignoring of terminal pauses at the location of psychological transitions destroys any chance of recreating a realistic thought pattern leading to the arc of the speech.

We became familiar with intoned pauses and terminal pauses when we studied sentences and punctuation: an intoned pause is longer than a micropause and is involved with a punctuation mark, and a terminal pause follows the end of a sentence, providing an opportunity for transitions of thought. And all of this, we know by now, is flexible and under the actor's control. The lengths of the intoned pauses created by punctuation, and the varied lengths of the transitional moments between sentences, are all fully under the actor's control. There is no set length to the pause and intonation from a semicolon's presence, for example; nor is there any preset limit to a terminal, transitional pause. Intoned and terminal pauses can vary almost infinitely in tone, in duration, and in their functions as well, which range from providing breathing space to the actor to endowing her with the power to string together printed and memorized thoughts into a living and believable performance. As protons and neutrons are to matter, so are patterns of widely varied stresses and the distribution of resonating spaces the constituent particles making up the universe of human communication.

THE POWER OF THE MICROPAUSE

But however valuable the longer pauses may be, it is the **micropause**—the neutrino of speech, to continue the nuclear metaphor—tiny and barely detectable, that is surprisingly useful to the actor, serving several quite distinct functions. These barely-a-breath pauses are usually called **"caesural"** pauses, but I prefer micropause because the term "caesural pause" carries no real information or guidance to the actor, whereas terms like "end-stopped," "enjambed," "*gravis*," or "operative" helpfully dictate their functions. "Micropause" is a much better verbal metaphor for this very useful tool, reminding us by its name of both its power and its brevity.

Micropauses are often too short to allow a breath and can't hold an intoned vowel or a change of tone, but what they can do is remarkable. These verbal neutrinos can:

- herd words together into small groups called "phrases";
- connect phrases to each other to form verse lines;
- split a ten-beat line into two parts, allowing the actor to explore more realistic speech patterns;
- provide a "touch of thought" to the end of an enjambed line.

When you speak in life, constructing your thoughts as you go along, micropauses give your lightning-fast mind the chance it needs to grab words for the next part of the sentence. Micropauses are also called "sense pauses," making clear one of their main functions: to act as an organizer of the parts of a thought, but doing so as the thought flows freely from the mouth. In the United Kingdom, they are sometimes called "magic pauses" in recognition of their power. Understanding the role of micropauses in spoken verse text is essential for the creation of a truthful and personally committed character. **Using pauses actively allows the actor to discover a living pattern of phrasing and pace that imposes a Stanislavskian reality onto a Shakespearean structure.**

THE PHRASE AND MIDLINE BREAK TOOL

The phrase part of the tool is very simple, but essential, knowledge: **Anglo-American English speakers tend to group their words into phrases of three to five words.** These phrases are linked by micropauses. This helps the actor handle a line or lines that have no internal punctuation. Punctuation forces strong phrasing: when a comma appears midline, we're "forced" to acknowledge that with a pause and, most likely, an upward or curling inflection. Since the line is likely ten beats, and ten beats can carry lots of words, that midline punctuation mark is forcefully dividing the line into two phrases. In that sense, the mark is operating not just as a phrasing pause, but as a midline break as well. They are not the same, although they are both allied with the micropause. A phrasing micropause separates small groups of words from one another, but a midline break specifically occurs at the rough midpoint of a line of verse, which is around the fourth, fifth, or sixth beat of the ten-beat line. This midline break can be an intoned pause from punctuation, or a micropause for phrasing. But its function is more specific than the general function of the phrasing pause.

When an actor is dealing with groups of lines that aren't punctuated, the actor needs to find natural but subtle phrasing pauses through oral reading. These tiny pauses, discovered as the material is said, must be allowed to enter into the reading of the text. Finding those tiny pause-beats in unpunctuated lines is essential because the structure of poetic drama requires that it be sounded out: **verse drama needs to be heard in order to exist.** This gives performed material a distinctly different life from material that is read or written. **It is not just sound that is heard and noted, but the absences of sound as well.** Without the phrasing pauses and the other micro- and longer pauses, the "sound" of the language rings false. The actor needs to investigate how micropauses can help phrase complex thoughts, and where they might be very useful—even essential— as a midline tool for handling unwieldy, unpunctuated lines of verse.

The reason midline breaks, whether punctuated or micro, are essential is that they are literally built into Shakespeare's verse. At the time Shakespeare was writing his earlier plays, placing a micropause after the fourth beat was all the rage. One of the greatest of Shakespearean meter studies puts it this way: "Tudor poetry treated the iambic pentameter line as the sum of two phrases, the first of four syllables, the second of six . . . for such an art, the phrase is clearly subordinate to the line. Among all the English phrases that occur to the poet as suitable to his other-that-metrical purposes, the poet must search for those that fit not only the iambic mold but also the four-six pattern as well."[2]

And in addition to that parameter, we should recall George Gascoigne's point: great poets choose their words so that the words' syllables carry the meter in a realistic, not consciously poetic, diction. The aim of theatrical blank verse is not a tortured, poetic construction, but a construction designed to imitate life in all its rhythmical, stressful, and tonal ways.

Here's a sample from *Richard III* that displays the fourth-beat micropause. I've pointed out the midline breaks with an asterisk (and the word "fleshed" is pronounced, as is often the case in Shakespeare, "flesh-ed"). Read it out loud, experimenting with the micropaused structure, and keep in mind that the pauses, unless punctuated, are **micro** . . . truly small!

---

2. George T. Wright, "The Play of Phrase and Line In Shakespeare's Iambic Pentameter," in *Shakespeare Quarterly* (Vol. 34, No. 2), 147.

> The tyrannous*and bloody act is done,
> The most arch deed*of piteous massacre
> That ever yet*this land was guilty of.
> Dighton and Forrest, who I did suborn
> To do this piece*of ruthful butchery,
> Albeit they were*flesh-ed villains, bloody dogs,
> Melted with tenderness*and mild compassion
> Wept like to children*in their deaths' sad story.

If you drive through the lines with purpose, always working to make the point of the sentence, you'll likely note that a tiny break at the asterisk allows you to do interesting things with balancing, or opposing, the phrases. And you are free to take this pause or that, suiting your feelings, as long as you don't evolve a pattern that is not phrased at all. So, fortuitously, the midline break, if taken, automatically phrases the line. But this piece of text is also useful to illustrate the tendency for phrasing in spoken English to break into small groups of three to five words. Here is the sample again, and note the numbers to the left: they are the numbers of words in the phrases that appear when the midline break is added.

> The tyrannous*and bloody act is done, (2/5)
> The most arch deed*of piteous massacre (4/3)
> That ever yet*this land was guilty of. (3/5)
> Dighton and Forrest, who I did suborn (3/4)
> To do this piece*of ruthful butchery, (3/4)
> Albeit they were*flesh-ed villains, bloody dogs, (3/4)
> Melted with tenderness*and mild compassion (3/3)
> Wept like to children*in their deaths' sad story. (3/5)

These structuring parameters of blank verse—a midline break, a coagulation of lines of words into shorter phrases—are not restrictions. Rather, they are guidelines crafted from our daily experiences in communicating with speech: we all phrase as we speak, as easily as we stress and in tone. Shakespeare structured these remarkable insights regarding natural speech into the text, relying on his actors' knowledge of how to handle verse like his. His goal is always to display character, and very rarely to show off: even then, it's the character showing off, not him.

TRY THIS . . .

Here's another sample from *Richard III*. Explore the lines out loud and on paper, and spot the micropauses hiding in the lines. Examine the phrases created by adding the tiny pause. And remember what we said at the start of the book about enjambed and end-stopped lines: **there is only a micropause at the end of an enjambed line**, a line with no punctuation at its end. Since there is no punctuation to stop the line, the micropause at the end of the enjambed line serves as a phrase pause, linking the last phrase of one line to the first phrase of the next.

> So now prosperity begins to mellow
> And drop into the rotten mouth of death.
> Here in these confines slyly have I lurked
> To watch the waning of mine enemies.
> A dire induction am I witness to,
> And will to France, hoping the consequences
> Will prove as bitter, black, and tragical.

As he matured as a playwright and experimented widely, Shakespeare began to play around with the concept of the midline break. He began to move it further up the line of ten beats, so that, eventually, it could be found as far as the seventh beat into the line. He combined that with more enjambed lines, so that the lines spoken by the great but often tortured characters of the later plays seem to be speeding, racing out of the characters' mouths, and have to be forcibly stopped with punctuation. The meter and sound of language in the later plays seem to reflect their complex, and in many cases, tortured psychologies, speeding along almost wildly, so that the hard stops of punctuation can actually jar us.

> The effects achievable by pausing late in the line had hardly been tried. Shakespeare tried them. They attracted him so much that eventually he seemed to be getting close to the point of giving up the first-half pauses altogether . . . when such a pause comes after the seventh, or even the eighth, syllable, the remaining space suffices only for a fragmentary statement which needs to be completed in the next line. In other words, very late pauses make for a run-on technique.[3]

---

3. Oras, 15–16.

Here's an example from *Timon of Athens* (1608) that shows this powerful, run-on energy. Compare this to the sample above from *Richard III* (1591), with its oddly calm and seemingly much shorter lines. These lines are spoken by Timon:

> Thou art a slave whom Fortune's tender arm
> With favor never clasped, but bred a dog.
> Hadst thou, like us from our first swath, proceeded
> The sweet degrees that this brief world affords
> To such as may the passive drudges of it
> Freely command, thou wouldst have plunged thyself
> In general riot; melted down thy youth
> In different beds of lust; and never learned
> The icy precepts of respect, but followed
> The sugared game before thee.

As Hans Oras writes, "After a line has achieved a certain momentum . . . a pause . . . cutting into the vigorous rhythmical movement, strikes the reader or listener with greater unexpectedness and seems more emphatic."[4] Here are some lines of Timon's from the same scene as the speeding lines above (3.2): these lines jolt with their vicious tone and fragmentary format.

> . . . The earth's a thief
> That feeds and breeds by a composture stol'n
> From general excrement. Each thing's a thief.
> The laws, your curb and whip, in their rough power
> Has unchecked theft. Love not yourselves. Away!
> Rob one another—there's more gold. Cut throats.
> All that you meet are thieves. To Athens go,
> Break open shops, nothing can you steal
> But thieves do lose it. Steal less for this I give you,
> And gold confound you howso'ere. Amen.

PHRASING AND UNPUNCTUATED LINES

Phrasing gives the actor the key to handling long sentences made up of lines with little or no internal punctuation. Now that we know what micropauses are, and that they can appear as a midline break or as that tiny breath-of-thought at the end of an enjambed line, let's look at how micropauses help us phrase a speech for which punctuation offers

---

4. Ibid., 16.

no help. Remember that the midline break is a phrase pause as well; it's a micropause serving two functions at once: one in a special place and with a special role.

In the sample from *RIII* that we looked at above, we counted the words of the phrases that emerged from applying the micropauses and we noted that, indeed, as research shows, most of the phrases were three to five words. Of course, this is not a rule, but a tool: it is to guide the actor, not shackle her. It alerts us to the need to phrase, to the opportunities of phrasing, and it provides us with a method: micropauses create the phrases, and the actor's work is linking the phrases—now distinct parts of a thought— into a whole idea, powerfully transmitted. The phrasing provides a through-line of sense to the arrangement of the words. Breath is essential for obvious reasons, most especially that real people breathe as they speak: actors new to Shakespeare or other metrical writing often don't.

12

The End of the Line Tool

*Provide the last beat of the line with energy: don't let
the line weaken near its end. The last beat of each line
connects to the first beat of the next line; the last word of a line
is often a verb, name, key word, or resolution of meaning,
all of which benefit from or require the application of stress;
or it may be punctuated, each mark of which
requires verbal energy of some type.*

Recalling an earlier discussion about enjambed and end-stopped lines, let's remind ourselves that an **enjambed** line of verse has no punctuation at the end of it, and was therefore meant to "jam" into the next line without a long pause. An **end-stopped** line, on the other hand, being halted in its flow by punctuation, takes an intoned pause. But the micropause at the end of an enjambed line is not meant to be taken as a noticeable pause, as is so clearly the case when pauses come from punctuation. This is a very important point! Taking any length of pause beyond a micropause at the end of unpunctuated lines introduces a jog-trot rhythm to which the audience can tap their feet. As Shakespearean teacher Barry Edelstein puts it:

> Throughout Shakespeare, characters do their thinking at line ends. These endings carve out space for the briefest interval of thought—a trick, a trice, a jiffy, a flash, a twinkle—in which the character's brain comes up with the next chunk of language the character will use. . . . It does not mean taking a long moment to ponder, cogitate, ruminate, and decide. . . . It does not mean rattling through every five-iamb line at a clip and stopping short at each line ending. . . . It does not mean falling into a mechanical, metronomic rhythm in which artful hesita-

tions at the end of the lines come so regularly that the audience member could set his watch by them.[1]

Here are some of the main reasons for carrying energy to the end of the line:

- the end of the line will often contain the word or words that make the point of the line;
- this is all the more true if the line is an entire sentence;
- often, lines end with verbs, which are happy to take a bit of stress;
- often, the last strong beat will be the second, resolving part of an antithesis, earning its own strong stress for that reason;
- sometimes, the punctuation at the end of the line dictates a strong stress and possibilities of intonation quite clearly, like a Q-mark (?) or an Ex-point (!);
- it's also a dee-DUM thing: that end word or phrase will contain the final strong beat of the line, since the regular iambic frame calls for ten beats of a dee-DUM pattern;
- since the meter of any line continues onto the next line or sentence, that line or sentence will likely (of course, not always) begin with a lesser stressed beat (dee-DUM), so the strong end-line stress in one line links it to the opening of the next line, maintaining the flow of energy in the meter.

Here are some lines that benefit from readings that carry energy to their ends, and for all the reasons above: they are the opening lines of *Twelfth Night*, spoken by Orsino:

> If music be the food of love, <u>play on,</u>
> Give me excess of it, that <u>surfeiting,</u>
> The appetite may sicken and so <u>die.</u>

- Each of the lines ends with a verb and a comma, urging us onto the next line;
- the lines build up an antithesis between "food" as nourishing in proper amounts, and food as something that surfeits and kills through excess;
- commas end the first two lines, carrying with them the notable upward inflections inherent in commas;

---

1. Barry Edelstein, *Thinking Shakespeare* (New York: Spark Publishing, 2007), 157.

- and, of course, there's the ever present dee-DUM, dee-DUM rhythm, with the last beat in the DUM position.

And here's Hamlet's famous musing, from 3.1:

> . . . Who would fardels bear,
> To grunt and sweat under a weary life
> But that the dread of something after death
> (The undiscovered country from whose bourn
> No traveler returns) puzzles the will
> And makes us rather bear those ills we have
> Than fly to others that we know not of?

There are lots of things to take note of here, especially when looking for reasons to carry energy to the end of the line. First, note that almost all of these lines are enjambed, meaning that only tiny pauses—phrasing micropauses—will appear at the ends of the lines, as each line barrels on to the next, connecting into one sentence. Then, note that there is no internal punctuation to speak of: that means you'll need to look for midline breaks and other phrasing opportunities. **There are nine verbs in the sentence:** each of them needs a bit of stress, and those stresses give you the energy to move on down the line toward the end, and toward the enjambed jump. In addition, the verbs are distributed throughout the sentence. **And note the parentheses!** That means the subthought is being dropped into the sentence with no intent to stop the flow of the thought; it's the double dashes—like this—that would slow the sentence down, so the injection of the parenthetical remark actually lightens the line and picks it up a bit, helping to keep the lines moving. There are so many reasons to carry the energy to the ends of the lines, if only to leap from the end of one to the beginning of the next.

In fact, there is rarely a justification for ending a line weakly. The great director of Shakespeare, Peter Hall, points out that:

> Most of Shakespeare's verse, early and late, is weighted at the end of the line. Seventy percent of his verse has the crux, or the important meaning, in the last words of the line. To drop the end of the line (or to allow it to droop in the depressed inflections of modern . . . English) usually produces a line with little meaning and no impact.[2]

---

2. Peter Hall, *Shakespeare's Advice to the Players* (New York: Theatre Communications Group, 2003), 28.

Other expert Shakespeare teachers agree. As voice expert Patsy Rodenburg puts it:

> When spoken properly, the verse line sounds quite different from prose not only because of the iambic rhythm, but because there is a sustained vocal energy through the line. It starts with a kick and ends with a held focus, like a laser beam from beginning to end. This energy represents the urgent heightened content that has been formally shaped into verse.[3]

Among the many reasons for the use of verse at all is to aid in memorization: the final heavy-stress word of a line or sentence gives the actor energy to push the lines forward. And this was something that not only the actors expected from their fellow actor and author Shakespeare, but the audience did as well. Shakespeare's contemporaries, which is to say, his audiences, "who conducted most of their business orally, were adept at listening. They were highly attentive to key words which would lead them in the direction the speaker was headed and connect the coming thought to the previous one."[4]

Other writers on Shakespearean performance also stress this point: "The actor must support the verse line all the way through to the final word. . . . **It is so important, because the natural speech of American actors is dramatically opposed to this necessary skill.**"[5]

> Supporting the last word or syllable in a blank verse line is not easy, and, once learned, is easily ignored. Physiologically, our diaphragm doesn't want to work that way. The muscle is "lazy" and prefers relaxation to tension. During voice training, actors learn to support speech. But even after training, many actors forget. . . . They forget for three reasons: 1) the effort to read the line "naturally" and truthfully encourages us to fade out at the end, 2) we don't practice speaking blank verse on a daily basis, and 3) breath support becomes lackadaisical, so rather than support the end of lines, it is easier to allow them to fade away like they do in our daily speech . . . any effort to support the ends of lines may at first seem strange or "overdone." But supporting is correct. If you don't support the end of the verse line, one can project that your Shakespeare will not be clear of truthful. The listener won't quite know what you are saying.[6]

---

3. Patsy Rodenburg, *Speaking Shakespeare* (New York: Palgrave Macmillan, 2002), 103.
4. Louis Fantasia *Instant Shakespeare* (Chicago: Ivan R. Dee, 2002), 68.
5. Wesley Van Tassle, *Clues to Acting Shakespeare* (New York: Allworth Press, 2000), 33.
6. Ibid., 34.

Ants Oras, who conducted a magisterial study in 1960 in which he analyzed every pause in all of Shakespeare and half a dozen other Elizabethan playwrights, concluded that during most of Shakespeare's early and middle career, he followed the usual pattern of midline breaks: a pause after beat four or five as standard practice. But in his later years, **he pushes the pause up to beat six, seven, or even eight**. The result was that **the end of the line was even more the object of all of the accumulating energy,** and withholding that pause drove the line on to the end with a tremendous burst. Yet, "Shakespeare's prevailing method in the later plays is not to provide a deviant metrical style for his distinctive characters, but to write a standard verse speech for each play and let the character's utterances vary from it according to their degrees of distress, anger or agitation."[7]

Try This . . .

Go back up to the Clifford speech in the Antithesis section, and this time, use it to explore what happens when you carry energy to the lines' ends. Most are end-stopped, which means they will almost certainly take a strong stress at the line end, since you'll need the energy for the intonation and forward movement of the thought. When you are done walking down Antithesis Way, try it again for end-of-line investigation. As has been noted, each pair of lines Clifford speaks is an antithesis; the last word of the first line will set up the second half of the antithesis in the next line. The first line of each pair ends with an interrogative mark, the Q-mark, and we almost always add extra energy to the final word of a question when we ask one in real life and make that punctuation sign with intonations. We do that to prime the answer that will follow, either from someone else if we are really asking them something, or from ourselves if we are using the questions rhetorically, as Clifford is.

"In all cases, the energy of the line is "harnessed on the last word."[8] Of course, breath is important here. Early on, I cited breathing as something that we use to support our own sentences; I mentioned that we never run out of breath under normal circumstances when we speak our own thoughts, since we instinctively use the breath we need to complete

---

7. George T. Wright, "Confessions of a Professional Meter Reader," in *Shakespeare Reread: The Text in New Contexts,* ed. Russ McDonald (Ithaca, NY and London: Cornell University Press, 1994), 57.
8. Op. cit., 105.

and properly stress or intone the thought. If we don't find the right pattern of breathing for a sentence or line, the energy runs out before we get to the ending, and it's not at all like what we do every day, when we speak and need to make our points effectively.

And here we are, at the end of the line. Here's a thought to help sum up our work:

> In preparing a speech, study the sentence and study the metrical line, and work out a way of speaking the words that is consistent with the stress requirements of both, that seems to spring from both, and that fits with your whole reading of the character and the dramatic situation. Then take advantage of your own voice and its special powers of timbre, volume, pitch, and pace to register nuance and expression.
>
> George T. Wright[9]

It's hard to sum things up better than that.

---

9. George T. Wright, "Troubles of a Professional Meter Reader," in *Shakespeare Reread: The Texts in New Contexts*, ed. Russ McDonald (Ithaca, NY: Cornell University Press, 1994), 67.

Brian A. Rose, PhD, is Professor of Acting in the Department of Theatre at Adelphi University. An actor with decades of experience in classical and modern performance, he is the author of *'Jekyll and Hyde' Adapted: Dramatizations of Cultural Anxiety* and holds degrees in dramatic literature, theatre theory/criticism, and theatre history. He has taught at Queens College (City University of New York), Cornell University's School of Labor Relations, and been performance guest artist at the University of Pittsburgh, Trinity University in San Antonio, and Ithaca College in Ithaca, New York.